PONS

W0270753

Gewusst wie!

Grammatik-Training
ENGLISCH 6. Klasse

Wer`s versteht, lernt leichter.

von
Birgit Piefke-Wagner

Ernst Klett Sprachen GmbH
Barcelona • Belgrad • Budapest • Ljubljana • London • Posen • Prag
Sofia • Stuttgart • Zagreb

PONS
Gewusst wie!

Grammatik-Training

ENGLISCH 6. Klasse

Wer`s versteht, lernt leichter.

von
Birgit Piefke-Wagner

Auflage A1 5 4 3 2 1 / 2010 2009 2008 2007

Internet: www.pons.de
E-Mail: info@pons.de

Redaktion: Debby Rebsch
Logoentwurf: Erwin Poell, Heidelberg
Logoüberarbeitung: Sabine Redlin, Ludwigsburg
Illustrationen: Stefan Theurer
Einbandgestaltung: Schmidt & Dupont
Titelfoto: Vlado Golub, Stuttgart
Layout/Satz: andrea grundmann kommunikationsgestaltung, Karlsruhe
Druck: Legoprint
Printed in Italy.
ISBN: 978-3-12-561383-6

Vorwort

Herzlich Willkommen!

Mit dem **PONS Gewusst wie! Grammatik-Training** hast du ein Übungsbuch, mit dem du gezielt bestimmte grammatische Themen wiederholen und üben kannst.

Wie ist das Buch aufgebaut?

Wir haben verschiedene grammatische Themen zu einem Themenblock zusammengefasst. Jeder Themenblock endet mit einem Test. Die **Kapitel** gehen meistens über zwei Seiten (manchmal auch über vier) und sind so aufgebaut, dass du auf der ersten (rechten) Seite die Erklärung zu einem Thema erarbeitest. Dann blätterst du um und wendest die Regeln zu diesem Thema in verschiedenen Übungen an, ohne die Erklärung zu sehen.
Im **Test** kannst du überprüfen, wie gut du die vorhergehenden Themen beherrschst. Im Anhang findest du die **Lösungen**, die **Wortliste,** in der du die wichtigsten englischen Wörter nachschlagen kannst, und eine Tabelle mit den **unregelmäßigen Verben**.

Dieses Symbol bedeutet ‚Achtung!' und weist dich auf Ausnahmen oder knifflige Sonderregeln hin. Diese Informationen sind besonders wichtig.

Hier findest du entweder einen Tipp zur Lösung der Übung oder einen weiterführenden Lerntipp.

Nicht alle grammatischen Themen, die hier behandelt werden, stehen in jedem Bundesland oder in jeder Schulart auch auf dem Lehrplan. Diese Themen oder Übungen haben wir mit einem Sternchen markiert.

Wie arbeitest du sinnvoll mit dem Buch?

Du kannst mit der **Bestandsaufnahme** beginnen, um auf die Schnelle zu sehen, welche Themen du noch üben solltest. Die Lösungen sagen dir, in welchem Kapitel das Thema bearbeitet wird. Oder du machst die Bestandsaufnahme am Schluss, um deine Fortschritte zu sehen.
Wenn du schon weißt, wo du mehr Übung brauchst, suchst du dir im **Inhaltsverzeichnis** gezielt Kapitel aus. Natürlich kannst du die Themen auch in der vorgegebenen Reihenfolge durcharbeiten.
Bei den Sternchenthemen und -übungen solltest du in deinem Schulbuch nachschauen, ob sie in diesem Schuljahr behandelt werden. Wenn ja, dann solltest du sie auf jeden Fall bearbeiten. Wenn sie für dich kein Thema sind, kannst du es trotzdem versuchen oder bis zum nächsten Schuljahr warten. Überspringe dann in den Tests die Sternchenübungen.

Viel Spaß und Erfolg beim Lernen!

Inhaltsverzeichnis

I

Inhaltsverzeichnis

I

Bestandsaufnahme

1 Ergänze mit question tags.
1. Ken is clever,
- a) is he? - b) isn't he?
- c) doesn't he?

2. Laura likes cats,
- a) does she? - b) is it? - c) doesn't she?

2 One oder ones?
Welches Stützwort passt hier? Schau mal die Pferde! Ich mag die braunen.
Look at the horses! I like
- a) the brown ones - b) the brown one.

3 Welches Beispiel zeigt die Steigerung eines Adjektivs?
- a) not as big as - b) big, bigger, the biggest - c) It isn't big.

4 Wie steigert man Adjektive mit drei Silben?
- a) Man kann sie nicht steigern.
- b) mit -er und -est
- c) mit more und most

5 Ein Adverb beschreibt
- a) ein Nomen näher - b) ein Verb näher - c) ein Subjekt näher

6 Die meisten Adverben unterscheiden sich von Adjektiven durch
- a) Großschreibung - b) nichts
- c) die Endung -ly

7 Welches Wort gehört in die Lücke?
1. I can speak English ________ .
a) good - b) well
2. Mary dances ________ .
- a) bad - b) badly
3. Martin has a ________ voice.
- a) nice - b) nicely

8 Welcher Satz ist richtig?
- a) My dad drives more carefully than my uncle.
- b) My dad drives more careful than my uncle.
- c) My dad drives most careful than my uncle.

9 Welche Präposition ist richtig?
1. vor dem Haus:
- a) before the house
- b) for the house
- c) in front of the house

2. hinter der Tür:
- a) under the door - b) behind the door - c) after the door

3. auf dem Tisch
- a) on the table - b) onto the table
- c) under the table

10 Was muss man bei der Schreibung von englischen Zahlen beachten?
- a) Tausender werden mit Komma geschrieben.
- b) Tausender werden mit Punkt geschrieben.
- c) Tausender werden groß geschrieben.

11 Some oder any? Welches Wort muss in die Lücke?
1. I haven't got ________ biscuits.
- a) some - b) any

2. Mark has got ________ good ideas.
- a) some - b) any

3. Could I have ________ milk, please?
- a) some - b) any

4. Sarah, have you got ________ money?
- a) some - b) any

B

Bestandsaufnahme

12 Welches Wort passt in den Satz?

1. My Dad knows ________________ about computers.
   - a) everybody
   - b) someone
   - c) everything
   - d) nowhere
2. Peter can't find his books ________________ .
   - a) everywhere
   - b) anywhere
   - c) somewhere
   - d) nowhere

13 Wenn du Wasser zum Trinken haben möchtest, fragst du

- a) Can I have water, please?
- b) Can I have a glass of water, please?
- c) Give me water, please.

14 Für Vermutungen, die im Englischen mit I think, I hope, I'm sure beginnen, braucht man

- a) will-future
- b) present progressive
- c) simple present

15 Welches Satzende ist richtig?

1. If we get a dog,
   - a) I'm walking with it every day.
   - b) I'll walk with it every day.
   - c) I walk with it every day.
2. Mum will make Pizza for us
   - a) if we watch the film at home.
   - b) if we are watching the film at home.
   - c) if we will watch the film at home.

16 In welcher Zeit steht die Frage Have you ever been to London?

- a) simple present
- b) present perfect
- c) present progressive

17 Welche fünf Verben sind unregelmäßig?

- 1. work
- 2. arrive
- 3. break
- 4. live
- 5. go
- 6. say
- 7. talk
- 8. tell
- 9. have

18 Welcher Satz enthält ein gerund?

- a) Tim is swimming.
- b) Tim likes swimming.
- c) Tim isn't swimming.

19 Für welches modal ist to have to die Ersatzform?

- a) may
- b) must
- c) can

20 Wie lautet ein Verb im past progressive?

- a) are singing
- b) sang
- c) was singing
- d) is singing

21 Ein Satz im going to future lautet

- a) We're going to Berlin by bus.
- b) We're going to go to Berlin by bus.
- c) We aren't going to Berlin by bus.

22 'Das sind Ihre.' heißt im Englischen

- a) They are yours.
- b) They are hers.
- c) They are theirs.

23 Welches Relativpronomen passt in den Satz

1. The CDs ________________ you gave me were great.
   - a) who
   - b) which
   - c) whose
2. The man ________________ asked me the way was very old.
   - a) who
   - b) which
   - c) whose
3. The woman ________________ keys we found was very happy.
   - a) who
   - b) which
   - c) whose

Grammatikbegriffe

adjective	Adjektiv (careful)
adverb	Adverb (carefully)
article, definite/indefinite	Artikel, bestimmter/unbestimmter (the/a,an)
auxiliary	Hilfsverb (be, do, have)
comparative	1. Steigerungsform (bigger, more careful)
conjunction/connective	Konjunktion,Bindewort (and, but, if, because, etc.)
contact clause	Relativsatz ohne Relativpronomen
future, will-future	Zukunft, Zukunft mit will
going to-future	Zukunft mit going to
gerund	Gerund(swimming, playing football)
s-genitive, of-genitive	s-Genitiv (my sister's friend), of-Genitiv (the title of the book)
imperative	Befehlsform, Imperativ
infinitive	Infinitiv, Grundform (1. Form)
modal	Modales Hilfsverb (can, must, mustn't, needn't)
noun	Substantiv, Nomen
cardinal numbers	Grundzahlen (1, 5, 12, 465, 1000, etc.)
ordinal numbers	Ordnungszahlen (1st, 2nd, 3rd, 4th, etc.)
object	Objekt (Wen oder was? Wem?)
past progressive	Verlaufsform der Vergangenheit
possessive pronoun	Possessivpronomen (mine, yours, etc.)
possessive determiner	Possessivbegleiter (my, your, etc)
preposition	Präposition (in, on, under, next to, in front of, etc.)
present perfect	Perfekt (have/has bought, have/has worked)
present progressive	Verlaufsform der Gegenwart
pronoun	Fürwort, Pronomen
object pronoun	Personalpronomen im Objektfall (me, him, etc.)
personal pronoun	Personalpronomen (I, you, he, she, it, we, you, they)
relative pronoun	Relativpronomen (who, which, that, whose)
question, question tags	Frage, Frageanhängsel / Bestätigungsfrage
question word	Fragewort (what, where, who, when, why, how)
relative clause	Relativsatz
sentence	Satz
short answer	Kurzantwort (Yes, I am. No, I'm not.)
simple past	einfache Vergangenheit, Imperfekt
simple present	einfache Gegenwart, Präsens
subject	Subjekt (Wer oder was?)
superlative	2. Steigerungsform (the biggest, the most careful)
verb, regular / irregular	Verb / Prädikat, regelmäßig (play, answer, ask, etc.) / unregelmäßig (be, go, tell, etc.)
word order	Wortstellung (S_V_O, Ort vor Zeit)

Question tags

Wollen wir in einem Gespräch Zustimmung oder Bestätigung, benutzen wir im Englischen question tags, sogenannte Bestätigungsfragen oder Frageanhängsel. Im Deutschen entsprechen sie dem ‚nicht wahr?' oder ‚stimmt's'?
Auf question tags erwartet man in der Regel keine Antwort.

1

Question tags bei Hilfsverben
Verbinde die Aussagesätze links mit den passenden question tags rechts.

1. The team is nervous, — c)
2. Mum, we aren't too late,
3. You've got a brother,
4. Kim wasn't at school,
5. Your dad is a teacher,
6. The Nelsons haven't got much money,

a) was she?
b) haven't you?
c) isn't it?
d) are we?
e) have they?
f) isn't he?

Ist das Prädikat im Aussagesatz bejaht (+), wird das Frageanhängsel verneint (-).
Ist das Prädikat im Aussagesatz verneint (-), wird das Frageanhängsel bejaht (+).

2

Question tags bei Vollverben
Verbinde die Aussagesätze links mit den passenden question tags rechts.

1. You like Norah Jones, — b)
2. Nina missed the bus,
3. Your brother plays the guitar,
4. Nick didn't pass the test,

a) didn't she?
b) don't you?
c) did he?
d) doesn't he?

Ist kein Hilfsverb im Aussagesatz, muss man für das Frageanhängsel je nach Person und Zeitform do, does, did oder don't, doesn't, didn't verwenden.

Question tags

3 Tina und Nicky bewundern die neue amerikanische Austauschschülerin Victoria. Sie ist mit ihrem Bruder für zwei Monate in Deutschland. Vervollständige die Aussagesätze mit den passenden question tags.

hasn't she · wasn't he? · isn't she? · doesn't he? · aren't they? · did she? · didn't we? · have they?

1. **Tina:** Look, there's Victoria. She's the girl from America, ______________________ ?
2. **Nicky:** She's got a nice brother, ______________________ ?
3. **Tina:** We met them in that new cafe yesterday, ______________________ ?
4. **Nicky:** Yes, but she didn't talk to you, ______________________ ?
5. **Tina:** The boy next to her was her brother, ______________________ ?
6. **Nicky:** He always smiles, ______________________ ?
7. **Tina:** I think her clothes are very nice, ______________________ ?
8. **Nicky:** Let's invite them to our next party. They haven't got many friends here, ______________________ ?
9. **Tina:** Good idea.

4 Vervollständige die folgenden Dialoge mit question tags.

1. **Julie:** Look at Sarah's new dress. It's lovely, ______________________ ?
   Helen: And look at her shoes. They're beautiful, ______________________ ?
2. **Mr Brown:** The Meyer's bought a new car, ______________________ ?
   Mr Miller: But they didn't buy a Porsche, ______________________ ?
3. **Teacher:** Kevin. Good morning. Look at your watch. It's 9 o'clock. You're late, ______________________ ?
   Kevin: Sorry, Mr Burton. I missed the bus.
   Teacher: That's right. And you missed an English lesson, ______________________ ?
   Kevin: I'm sorry.

One/ones

2

1 Setze one oder ones ein.

1. I've got two budgies in my room, a blue ________ and a yellow ________ .
2. Our neighbours have got two cars, a new ________ and an old ________ .
3. Can I have one of your new CDs, please? Yes, of course, which ________ would you like?
4. Mum, which shoes are clean? The black ________ ? Mum: No, they're still dirty.

Wenn man in einem Gespräch ein zählbares Substantiv nicht wiederholen möchte, kann man es im Englischen durch das Stützwort ________ (Singular) oder ________ (Plural) ersetzen.
One/ones kann auch nach the, this, that, these, those oder bei Fragen nach which stehen. Es ersetzt auch hier ein zählbares Substantiv.

2 Verbinde die englischen Ausdrücke mit den deutschen Bedeutungen.

1. the short one or the long one
2. the brown ones
3. Which one is yours?
4. an expensive one and two cheap ones
5. Which ones are the best?

a) die braunen
b) Welche sind die besten?
c) ein teures und zwei billige
d) das Kurze oder das Lange
e) Welches gehört dir?

Das Stützwort one, ones wird nicht übersetzt!

One/ones

3 Ergänze die Lücken mit which one/which ones.

1. Fünf Mäntel! Welcher ist deiner?
   Five coats, ___which one___ is yours?
2. Drei Rucksäcke! Welchen brauchst du?
   Three rucksacks, ______ do you need?
3. Zwei Sitzplätze! Welchen hättest du gerne?
   Two seats, ______ would you like?
4. So viele Bonbons! Welche darf ich essen?
   So many sweets! ______ can I eat?

4 Setze das entsprechende Adjektiv und das Stützwort one oder ones ein.

1. **Woman:** I'm looking for some new jeans. Have you got any (*billige*) ______ ______ ?
   Shop assistant: You can try these (*blauen*) ______ . They're not too expensive.
2. My brother has got two little mice in his room, a (*graue*) ______ and a (*weiße*) ______ .
3. **Susan:** Hey, Karen, can you see the two women in front of the shop over there? The (*große*) ______ is my English teacher and the (*mit dem Hut*) ______ is my PE teacher.

Adjektive: Steigerung auf *-er* und *-est*

1 Unterstreiche alle Adjektive, auch die 1. und die 2. Steigerungsform:

1. Dad is quite old, but Mum is older than Dad, and Grandpa is the oldest person in our family.
2. Mrs Brown is a nice teacher. Mrs White is nicer. Mr Black is the nicest teacher.
3. It's hot in Italy. It's hotter in Spain. The hottest countries are in Africa.
4. English is easy. German is easier. Maths is the easiest subject at school.

Bei der ______________________ der meisten einsilbigen Adjektive und manchen zweisilbigen Adjektiven wird an das Adjektiv ______________ oder ______________ angehängt.

Besondere Schreibweise:

nic**e**	nic**er**	(the) nic**est**	(das **e** wird nicht verdoppelt)
ho**t**	ho**tt**er	(the) ho**tt**est	(das **t** wird verdoppelt)
happ**y**	happ**i**er	(the) happ**i**est	(aus **y** wird **i**)

Es gibt auch Adjektive mit unregelmäßiger Steigerung:

good	better	(the) best
bad	worse	(the) worst

2 Vergleicht man Personen, Dinge oder Handlungen miteinander, ergeben sich folgende Mögklichkeiten:

as big **as** – **so** groß **wie**
not as big **as** – **nicht so** groß **wie**
(not) bigger **than** – (nicht) größer **als**

th**a**n = als! (beim Vergleich)
th**e**n = dann, danach!

3 Ergänze die folgenden Sätze sinnvoll.

the best – ~~bigger~~ – older – ~~younger~~
not as cheap as – ~~easier~~ – poorer – as big as

1. Berlin is ______________ than Cologne. 2. Teenagers are ______________ than 20. 3. A computer is ______________ a mobile phone. 4. This exercise is ______________ than the exercises on the next page. 5. ______________ subject at school is PE. 6. Many people in Africa are ______________ than people in Europe. 7. Spain is almost ______________ France. 8. Mum is ______________ than me.

Adjektive: Steigerung auf *-er* und *-est*

4 a) Fülle die Lücken aus. Achte auf besondere Schreibweisen!

Grundform	1. Steigerungsform	2. Steigerungsform
1. **nice** ______	______	(the) ______
2. ______	______	(the) **cleanest**
3. ______	**dirtier**	(the) ______
4. ______	**hotter**	(the) ______
5. **high** ______	______	(the) ______
6. ______	______	(the) **easiest**

b) Übersetze die fett gedruckten Wörter aus 4 a) ins Deutsche.

1. ______ 2. ______

3. ______ 4. ______

5. ______ 6. ______

5 Setze das Adjektiv in der richtigen Form (Grundform oder 1. oder 2. Steigerungsform) ein.

1. Tim is very good at computers. He's cleverer than our teacher. (*clever*)
2. I'm not very good at German, but my last German test was ______ than Kim's test. (*good*)
3. Nicole's parents gave her a dog for her birthday. She's the ______ girl in town. (*happy*)
4. Last Wednesday we had –15°C. That was the ______ day in February. (*cold*)
5. My best friend Susie won the song competition last Sunday. I'm so ______ of her. (*proud*)
6. It's sometimes much ______ to talk to friends than to talk to sisters. (*easy*)
7. Mum, can you drive me to school, please? I don't want to be ______ than the others. (*late*)
8. A lot of pupils in my class are twelve. Valentin is eleven. He's the ______.(*young*)

Adjektive: Steigerung mit *more* und *most*

1 Ordne die folgenden Adjektive nach Silbenanzahl und schreibe sie in die Tabelle. Kennst du auch die Bedeutung dieser Adjektive?

stupid good late expensive interesting beautiful great difficult dangerous boring ~~quick~~ nice famous careful brilliant

einsilbig	zweisilbig	dreisilbig
English	English	English
quick		

2 Unterstreiche die mehrsilbigen Adjektive und die Steigerungsformen.

1. Dad is careful. Mum is more careful. My brother is the most careful driver in our family.
2. France is beautiful. Spain is more beautiful. Ireland is the most beautiful country in the world.

Bei der ______________ aller drei- und mehrsilbigen Adjektive und den meisten zweisilbigen Adjektiven wird dem Adjektiv ______________ oder ______________ vorangestellt.

3 Vergleicht man Personen, Dinge oder Handlungen miteinander, ergeben sich folgende Möglichkeiten:

than = als! (beim Vergleich)
then = dann, danach!

as dangerous **as** – **so** gefährlich **wie**
not as dangerous **as** – **nicht so** gefährlich **wie**
(not) more dangerous **than** – (nicht) gefährlicher **als**

Adjektive: Steigerung mit *more* und *most*

4 Ein-, zwei- und dreisilbige Adjektive. Schreibe die Steigerungsformen auf.

Grundform	1. Steigerungsform	2. Steigerungsform
1. popular	______________________	______________________
2. famous	______________________	______________________
3. good	______________________	______________________
4. sunny	______________________	______________________
5. long	______________________	______________________
6. careful	______________________	______________________
7. bad	______________________	______________________
8. interesting	______________________	______________________

5 Stelle Vergleiche an.

1. A house is ______________________ (*größer als*) a garage.
2. The girls in our class are ______________________ (*so intelligent wie*) the boys.
3. Thomas Gottschalk is ______________________ (*berühmter als*) Kai Pflaume.
4. My sister Jennifer is ______________________ (*schlauer als*) my brother.
5. Music on a cassette is ______________________ (*nicht so gut wie*) music on a CD.

6 Übersetze die Sätze ins Deutsche.

1. The weather in Great Britain is not as nice as in Spain.

____

____

2. My best friend is 12 and I'm 12, too. So he is as old as I am.

____

____

1 Ergänze mit question tags.

1. Teachers aren't always nice, ________________________?
2. You are German, ________________________?
3. Your sister has got a boyfriend, ________________________?
4. You eat vegetables, ________________________?
5. Kevin took the money from the desk, ________________________?
6. Tina Meyers was in your class, ________________________?

2 Übersetze die unterstrichenen Satzteile.

1. Can you see the girls over there? <u>The one with red hair</u> is my new friend.

____

2. Look at the bikes. <u>The new one is mine.</u>

____

3. This poster is great. Yes, <u>but those ones over there</u> are cool, too.

____

4. We've got three cats, <u>a brown one and two black ones.</u>

____

3 Setze die 1. oder die 2. Steigerungsform ein.

1. I like Maya. She's much ________________ (*nice*) than the other girls.
2. Kim is new. He's the ________________ (*funny*) boy in our class.
3. Mum, don't look at my German test. I wrote the ________________ (*bad*) test.
4. I don't like sports, but football is ________________ (*good*) than basketball.
5. My brother is ________________ (*young*) than me but he is

   ________________ (*tall*) than me.

TIPP Die 2. Steigerungsform braucht immer ein the (big - bigger - <u>the</u> biggest).

4 Steigere die folgenden **Adjektive**.

Grundform	1. Steigerungsform	2. Steigerungsform
bad	______	______
hot	______	______
happy	______	______
careful	______	______

5 Sarah ist Fan einer berühmten Band und schwärmt von den Sängern. Übersetze.

1. Sie sind die beste Boygroup auf der Welt.

______

2. Sie sind die schönsten Tänzer.

______

3. Sie haben die verrücktesten Schuhe.

______

4. Sie sind die berühmtesten Jungs in Deutschland.

______

6 Übersetze und setze in den richtigen Satz ein.

so teuer wie – nicht so hoch wie – schwieriger als – viel größer als – der schlechteste – heißer als – nicht so schnell wie

1. A hill is ______ a mountain.
2. A bear is ______ a lion.
3. A mobile is ______ a camera.
4. Chinese is ______ English.
5. Germany is ______ Italy.
6. Yesterday it was ______ today.
7. Monday is ______ day of the week.

Adverbien auf *-ly* und unregelmäßige Adverbien

1 Hier geht es um den Unterschied zwischen Adjektiv und Adverb. Schreibe die Adverbformen auf.

	Adjektiv	Nomen		Verb	Adverb
1. Lucy is a	beautiful	singer.	She	sings	beautifully. ______.
2. Pete is a	quick	swimmer.	He	swims	______.
3. Sam is a	bad	tennis player.	He	plays	______.
4. Colin is a	slow	learner.	He	learns	______.
5. Dad is a	careful	driver.	He	drives	______.
6. This is a	nice	picture.	You	drew it	______.

Setze die folgenden Wörter richtig ein: *Tätigkeit*, *Adverb*, -y, *Person*, *Gegenstand*, -ly

Ein Adjektiv beschreibt eine ______ oder einen ______, also ein Nomen, näher. Ein ______ beschreibt eine ______, bzw. ein Verb näher. Aus vielen Adjektiven kann man ein Adverb bilden, indem man ______ anhängt. Bei Adjektiven, die auf ______ enden, lautet die Adverbendung -ily.

2 Folgende Adverbformen sind mit dem Adjektiv identisch: fast, hard, high, early, late. Übersetze die farbigen Adjektive und Adverben.

Adjektiv

1.a) He is a fast runner.

Er ist ein ______ Läufer.

2.a) This is a hard week.

Dies ist eine ______ Woche.

3.a) This is a high tower.

Dies ist ein ______ Turm.

Adverb

1.b) He runs fast.

Er läuft ______ .

2.b) We are working hard.

Wir arbeiten ______ .

3.b) You can jump high.

Du kannst ______ springen.

Besondere Adverbbildungen sind außerdem: terrible → terrib<u>ly</u>, fantastic → fantasti<u>cally</u>
Unregelmäßige Adverbformen sind: good → <u>well</u>

Adverbien auf *-ly* und unregelmäßige Adverbien

3 Schreibe die Adverbformen der folgenden Adjektive auf.

1. slow – ______________ 2. wonderful – ______________
3. bad – ______________ 4. right – ______________
5. quiet – ______________ 6. good – ______________
7. fast – ______________ 8. clear – ______________
9. nice – ______________ 10. angry – ______________

4 Fehlt hier ein Adjektiv oder ein Adverb? Setze die richtige Form ein.

1. We're (*lucky*) ______________ . We've got a very (*good*) ______________ English teacher. He speaks (*slow*) ______________ and (*clear*) ______________ .
2. Toby can dance very (*good*) ______________ . He can run (*quick*) ______________ , too.
3. My brother always eats (*slow*) ______________ . But he drinks (*fast*) ______________ .
4. Beyoncé sings (*beautiful*) ______________ . She has got a (*beautiful*) ______________ voice.
5. Can you carry the cake (*careful*) ______________ , please?
6. The next match is against a (*slow*) ______________ team. We can win (*easy*) ______________ .

TIPP: Wenn du dir nicht sicher bist, überlege was das Wort näher beschreibt: ein Verb oder ein Nomen?

5 Adjektiv oder Adverb? Übersetze ins Englische.

1. Du kannst gut schwimmen. ______________
2. Tim ist ein guter Freund. ______________
3. Valerie lachte glücklich. ______________
4. Kannst du bitte langsam sprechen? ______________
____
5. Mama fährt immer vorsichtig. ______________

Steigerung und Vergleiche mit Adverbien

6

1 Unterstreiche die Adverben und ihre Steigerungsformen und ergänze dann die Regel.

Peter eats fast. Becca eats faster, but Ben eats the fastest. Lucy eats slowly. Mike eats more slowly, but Grandma eats the most slowly.

Setze ein: *Adverbien*, -er, -est, *Endung*, more, most

Die Steigerung der Adverben folgt den gleichen Regeln wie die Steigerung der Adjektive:

Adverbien mit mehr als einer Silbe, das sind alle Adverbien mit der ______________ –ly, werden mit ______________ und ______________ gesteigert. Nur einsilbige ______________ werden wie einsilbige Adjektive mit ______________ und ______________ gesteigert.

2 Du kennst schon die unregelmäßige Steigerung der beiden Adjektive good und bad und ihre Adverbformen. Die Steigerungsformen dieser beiden Wörter sind für Adjektiv und Adverb gleich. Schreibe die Steigerungsformen in die Lücken.

Adjektiv:

good ________ ________ *bad* ________ ________

Adverb:

well ________ ________ *badly* ________ ________

3 Vergleiche mit Adverbien werden wie Vergleiche mit Adjektiven gebildet. Fülle die Lücken aus. Die deutsche Übersetzung kann dir helfen.

1. Sarah dances ________ beautifully ________ Luisa.

   Sarah tanzt **so** schön **wie** Luisa.

2. Kim speaks ________ clearly ________ Laura.

   Kim spricht deutlich**er als** Laura.

3. Melissa dances the ________ ________ .

   Melissa tanzt **am schönsten**.

Steigerung und Vergleiche mit Adverbien

4 Adjektiv oder Adverb?

TIPP Was wird genauer beschrieben? Wenn es das Nomen ist, dann musst du das Adjektiv auswählen. Wird das Verb näher beschrieben, dann wähle das Adverb aus.

Linda is a very (1) ____________________ (*nice / nicely*) girl. She is always friendly. She is very (2) ____________________ (*good / well*) at English, but she doesn't understand Maths very (3) ____________________ (*good / well*). I think she is (4) ____________________ (*cleverer / more cleverly*) than I am. We sometimes do our homework together. It's not (5) ____________________ (*easy / easily*) to work together (6) ____________________ (*quiet / quietly*). Linda always writes and draws her homework (7) ____________________ (*careful / carefully*) and her exercise books are (8) ____________________ (*tidier / more tidily*) than mine. I always finish my exercises (9) ____________________ (*quicker / more quickly*), but they are not as (10) ____________________ (*correct / correctly*) as Linda's. Linda has got a (11) ____________________ (*beautiful / beautifully*) dog, Baffy. He always barks (12) ____________________ (*loud / loudly*) when he sees her. He knows me (13) ____________________ (*good / well*). He's a (14) ____________________ (good / well) friend, too. But he never helps me with my homework.

5 Setze das richtige Wort in der Grundform oder einer Steigerungsform ein. Entscheide zuerst, ob es sich um ein Adjektiv oder ein Adverb handelt.

clear good slow good good fast

1. Could you drive (*langsamer*) ______________________________, please?
2. Could you speak (*deutlicher*) ______________________________, please?
3. I ran (*schneller*) ______________________________ than David in the last competition.
4. Your English is not (*schlecht*) ______________________________. You can speak English very (*gut*) ______________________________.
5. Thank you, but I can't speak English (*so gut wie*) ______________________________ you can.

Präpositionen

1 **Welches** Monster befindet sich **an welcher Stelle** in diesem Zimmer? Schreibe Sätze.

behind,
on
in
in front of
~~under~~

1. The green monster is under the bed.
2.
3.
4.
5.

2 Manche Präpositionen verbinden sich mit anderen Wörtern zu einem festen Ausdruck. Am besten lernst du solche Wendungen auswendig. Ergänze die englischen oder deutschen Ausdrücke mit der richtigen Präposition.

1. in der Schule – at school
2. ins Haus hinein – ______ the house
3. ______ Hause – at home
4. mit dem Zug – ______ train
5. bei der Arbeit – ______ work
6. nach Stuttgart – ______ Stuttgart

Manchmal ist im Englischen eine Präposition nötig, im Deutschen dagegen braucht man keine und umgekehrt:

Deutsch	Englisch	Beispiel
nach Hause	home	Let's go home.
2004	in 2004	They closed the cinema in 2004.

‚Nach Hause' steht im Englischen **ohne** Präposition: home. **‚Zu Hause'** steht im Englischen **mit** einer Präposition: at home.

Präpositionen

3 Lies die Sätze und male zu jedem Satz eine kleine Skizze.

1. There's a ball under the chair.
2. There's a ball next to the table.
3. There's a ball in the basket.
4. There's a ball between two chairs.
5. There's a ball on the table.
6. There's a ball behind the boy.

1.	2.	3.	4.	5.	6.

4 Setze Präpositionen ein.

before in front of next to before at to between after to

Sarah is going (1) ______________ the cinema with two friends. They meet (2) ______________ the cinema half an hour (3) ______________ the film starts. The film starts (4) ______________ 3 o' clock. Sarah wants to buy a drink and a bag of popcorn (5) ______________ the film. (6) ______________ the film the girls want to go (7) ______________ a takeaway. There's a takeaway (8) ______________ the cinema. The girls must be back home (9) ______________ 6 and 7 o'clock.

5 Ein paar Wendungen mit Präpositionen kennst du schon. Übersetze ins Englische und achte besonders auf die unterstrichenen Satzteile. Beachte auch die Wortstellung.

1. Wohin fährst du? Nach Frankfurt. ______________________________
2. Ich stehe um 6 Uhr am Morgen auf. ______________________________
3. Wir fahren mit dem Bus zur Schule. ______________________________
4. Meine Schwester ist auch in der Schule. ______________________________
5. Ich bin nie vor 12 Uhr zu Hause. ______________________________
6. Mein Vater ist bei der Arbeit. ______________________________

1 Lies den Text, unterstreiche die zehn Adjektive und fünf Adverbien und trage sie in die Tabelle ein.

Yesterday my good friend Mona visited me. She lives next to the little shop in Rock Street. She wanted to see my new rabbit. We opened the cage quietly and gave it some fresh, green lettuce. Then Mona wanted to hold it because it was so soft. I showed her how: You walk slowly towards it. Then you grab it firmly by its neck and lift it up carefully. Mona picked it up, but then it jumped down and hopped over the old fence into our neighbour's garden. We had to look for it quickly, because it was late. But we found it and put it back into its safe cage. Mona and I were happy because we found the rabbit again.

Adjektive		Adverbien

2 Welche der folgenden Wörter sind als Adjektiv und Adverb gleich?

wonderful angry right clear fast slow long perfect hard early

a) ____________ b) ____________ c) ____________ d) ____________ e)____________

3 Schreibe auf, was Mike alles gut kann und was er nicht so gut kann.

1. (*schnell laufen*) Mike can ____________________________
2. (*nicht schön singen*) Mike can't ____________________________
3. (*hart arbeiten*) ____________________________
4. (*nicht leise Gitarre spielen*) ____________________________
5. (*gut English sprechen*) ____________________________
6. (*glücklich lachen*) ____________________________

Test 2

4 Steigere die folgenden **Adverbien.**

Adverb	1. Steigerung	2. Steigerung
slowly		
beautifully		
fast		
carefully		

5 1. Steigere die **Adjektive** good und bad.

Adjektiv	1. Steigerung	2. Steigerung
good		
bad		

2. Wie heißen die **Adverbien** von good und bad? ____________ und ____________

3. Steigere nun die **Adverbien** von good und bad.

Adverb	1. Steigerung	2. Steigerung

6 Wie heißt es im Englischen richtig? Unterstreiche die korrekte Satzergänzung.

1. From Monday to Friday pupils have to go a) on school, b) at school, c) to school.
2. My family always has breakfast together a) in Saturdays, b) on Saturdays, c) at Saturdays.
3. My best friend's birthday is a) in May, b) on May, c) at May.
4. School in Germany starts a) before 9 o'clock, b) on 9 o'clock, c) next to 9 o'clock.
5. I always go to school a) in the bus, b) at the bus, c) by bus.

Zahlen

1 Schreibe die Zahlen aus der Zahlenpyramide in Worten: links Englisch, rechts Deutsch.

______ 100 ______

______ 1,000 ______

______ 10,000 ______

______ 100,000 ______

______ 1,000,000 ______

______ 1,000,000,000 ______

Setze die folgenden Wörter ein: and, a, *eine Milliarde, Punkt, Komma*

1. Englische Zahlen werden in **einzelnen** Wörtern geschrieben.
2. Zwischen Hundertern und Zehnern kann ein ______ stehen.
3. Vor hundred und thousand muss ein ______ stehen.
4. Bei Zahlen ab Tausend wird als Tausendertrennzeichen ein ______ gesetzt. In deutschen Zahlen steht als Tausendertrennzeichen ein ______.
5. Aufgepasst! One billion ist im Deutschen ______!

TIPP

Jahreszahlen spricht man so:
1995 – nineteen hundred and ninety-five oder: nineteen ninety-five
2008 – two thousand and eight

2 Verbinde die Schreibweisen mit den entsprechenden Zahlen.

1. eleven thousand two hundred and fifty-six	a) 7,893
2. four million eight hundred and sixty thousand three hundred and forty-one	b) 114
3. one hundred and fourteen	c) 11,256
4. forty-four thousand seven hundred and twenty-nine	d) 4,860,341
5. one hundred and one thousand five hundred and fifty-three	e) 44,729
6. seven thousand eight hundred and ninety-three	f) 794
7. seven hundred and ninety-five	g) 101,553

Zahlen

3 Kennst du dich mit Fakten gut aus? Wenn nicht, dann musst du raten. Schreibe die richtige Zahl in Ziffern in die Lücke. Denke an das richtige Tausendertrennzeichen.

seventy-five thousand | one thousand six hundred and nine | ten thousand | three hundred and sixty-five | three hundred and eighty-four thousand | ~~forty thousand~~ | eighty-six thousand four hundred | eight billion

1. It's ___40,000___ kilometres around the world.
2. ______ people can go to a concert in the Olympic stadium in Munich.
3. There are ______ seconds per day.
4. There are ______ grams in 10 kilograms.
5. One mile is ______ metres.
6. ______ people live on the earth.
7. There are ______ kilometres between the moon and the earth.
8. One year has got ______ days.

4 Schreibe auf, wie man die folgenden Zahlen spricht.

a) 111 ______

b) 444 ______

c) 7,279 ______

d) 12,388 ______

e) 212,767 ______

f) 1,897,413 ______

g) 3,800,500,200 ______

Some und *any* in Aussagen und Fragen

9

1 Verbinde die englischen Sätze mit der richtigen deutschen Übersetzung.

1. I want to invite some friends.
2. Have you got any ideas?
3. Have you got any money?
4. Sorry, I haven't got any money.
5. He is getting some drinks for us.

a) Tut mir leid, ich habe kein Geld.
b) Hast du Geld?
c) Habt ihr Ideen?
d) Er holt Getränke für uns.
e) Ich möchte ein paar Freunde einladen.

2 Trage die englischen Beispiele aus Übung 1 in die Tabelle ein.

Satzarten	Beispielsätze
Bejahte Sätze:	______________________ ______________________
Fragen:	______________________ ______________________
Verneinte Sätze:	______________________

3 Unterstreiche alle some und any in der Tabelle oben und vervollständige die Regel.

Setze ein: *ein paar,* some, any, *unbestimmte, verneinten, bejahten*

Im Englischen benutzt man __________ oder __________, um eine __________________

Menge oder Anzahl von etwas auszudrücken, im Deutschen sagt man **etwas, einige** oder

__________________. In __________________________ Sätzen setzt man dafür some ein,

in __________________ Sätzen und in Fragen meistens any. In manchen Fällen werden

some und any im Deutschen auch gar nicht übersetzt.

Es gibt Ausnahmen, wo man ein some in Fragen verwenden darf:
Would you like some tea? Möchten Sie (etwas) Tee?
Could you give me some money, please? Kannst du mir bitte (etwas) Geld geben?
Some in Fragen wählt man dann, wenn man ein höfliches **Angebot** oder eine höfliche **Bitte** aussprechen möchte.

Some und *any* in Aussagen und Fragen

4 Setze some oder any ein. Wenn du nicht sicher bist, überlege zuerst, ob es sich um einen bejahten Satz, einen verneinten Satz oder eine Frage handelt.

1. My sister can give you ______ tips for your trip to London.
2. Mum, have you got ______ biscuits? – Yes, there are ______ in the brown box.
3. I don't have ______ problems with my parents. They're great.
4. Did you get ______ money for the job? – No, I didn't get ______ money.
5. Have you got ______ interesting clubs at school? – Yes, we have ______ great clubs here.
6. Would you like ______ cornflakes for breakfast? – Yes, please.
7. Could I have ______ water, please? – Yes, of course. Here you are.

5 Verwandle die folgenden bejahten Aussagesätze in verneinte Aussagesätze.

1. Nick has got some brilliant ideas.
   Nick hasn't got any brilliant ideas.
2. Nora has got some stupid friends.
   Nora ______
3. Great, you bought some milk!
   Oh no, ______
4. I had some problems with the computer.
   ______

6 Übersetze ins Deutsche.

1. Have you got any news? ______
2. I don't need any hobbies. ______
3. We need some eggs for the cake. ______

Zusammensetzungen mit *some* und *any, every* und *no*

10

1 Hier sind alle Zusammensetzungen von some, any, every und no. Ergänze.

some**one**	any ________	every ________	no ________
some**body**	any ________	every ________	no ________
some**thing**	any ________	every ________	no ________
some**where**	any ________	every ________	no ________

2 Die Zusammensetzungen von some und any entsprechen den deutschen Bedeutungen **(irgend)jemand, (irgend)etwas, irgendwo**. Ordne die deutschen Wörter zu.

1. someone / somebody und anyone / anybody ________
2. something und anything ________
3. somewhere und anywhere ________

Setze ein: *verneinten*, some, any, *Zusammensetzungen, Fragen, bejahten*

Für die Verwendung der ________ von some und any gelten die gleichen Regeln wie für ________ und ________: Alle Zusammensetzungen mit some werden in ________ Sätzen verwendet, während alle Zusammensetzungen mit any in ________ Sätzen und ________ verwendet werden.

3 Die Zusammensetzungen von every heißen ins Deutsche übertragen: **alle** oder **jede/r, überall, alles**. Setze everybody, everywhere, everything in die Lücken.

1. My best friend knows ________ about German football players.
2. ________ knows that you mustn't feed animals at the zoo.
3. Joe, tidy up your room. There are clothes ________ .

4 Die Zusammensetzungen mit no heißen **nirgends, niemand, nichts**. Ordne die deutschen Wörter zu.

1. nobody = not anybody ________
2. nothing = not anything ________
3. nowhere = not anywhere ________

Zusammensetzungen mit *some* und *any*, *every* und *no*

5 Finde die passenden Ausdrücke und schreibe sie hinter die deutsche Übersetzung. Am besten merkst du dir solche nützlichen Wendungen als Ganzes.

1. Lasst uns jemanden fragen.

____

2. Noch etwas?

____

3. Was ist los? – Nichts.

____

4. Ich kannte keinen.

____

Anything else?
I didn't know anybody.
What's the matter? – Nothing.
Let's ask somebody.

6 Hier müssen sechs verschiedene zusammengesetzte Wörter eingesetzt werden. Welche?

1. Ich kann nichts sehen.	I can't see *anything.*
2. Ich kann niemanden sehen.	I can't see ______________
3. Ich kann jemanden sehen.	I can see ______________
4. Ich kann alles sehen.	I can see ______________
5. Ich kann etwas sehen.	I can see ______________
6. Ich kann alle / jeden sehen.	I can see ______________

7 Setze ein:

anywhere, anybody, nowhere, nobody, somebody, somewhere, everybody

Where are my shoes? I can't see them (1) ______________ . They must be (2) ______________ here in the house. Tom, Helen, has (3) ______________ seen my shoes? They are (4) ______________ . It's funny, (5) ______________ knows where my shoes are. (6) ______________ says, "I don't know." I need (7) ______________'s help. I can't leave the house without shoes!

Mengenangaben und nicht zählbare Substantive

11

1 Hier siehst du unterschiedliche Mengenangaben. Welche Mengenangaben drücken eine bestimmte Menge, welche eine unbestimmte Menge von etwas aus? Unterstreiche nur die Mengenangaben, trage sie in die Tabelle ein und übersetze sie. Achtung! Das of wird nicht mit übersetzt!

not much water, two bottles of milk, a glass of apple juice, some coffee, one bar of chocolate, a pound of butter, one glass of jam, two cups of tea, two tins of cat food, one packet of sugar, much money, a lot of information, no news, little water, a piece of cheese

bestimmte Mengenangaben (9)	unbestimmte Mengenangaben (6)
two bottles of – zwei Flaschen	*not much – nicht viel*

Manche englischen Substantive, vor allem Flüssigkeiten (z.B. tea, water), einige Lebensmittel (z.B. sugar, bread) und einige andere Begriffe (z.B. money, information) nennt man **nicht zählbar**, weil man kein a / an oder one, two, three, usw. davorsetzen kann. Für sie braucht man die Wendungen für bestimmte und unbestimmte Mengenangaben aus der Tabelle oben.

2 Vergleiche die englischen Sätze mit den deutschen. Was fällt Dir bei den Mengenangaben auf?

Have you got **any money**? Hast du **Geld**?

Let's buy **some chocolate**. Lass' uns **Schokolade** kaufen.

Im Deutschen können wir unbestimmte Mengenangaben vor Nomen weglassen, im Englischen nicht!

Mengenangaben und nicht zählbare Substantive

3 Übersetze ins Englische.

Das englische Wort information bleibt immer im Singular!!

1. zwei Gläser Orangenlimonade ______
2. etwas Zucker ______
3. eine Tüte Schokoladenkekse ______
4. keine neuen Informationen ______
5. vier Pfund frische Butter ______
6. nicht viel Geld ______

4 Richtig (✔) oder falsch (✘)? Kreuze an und korrigiere die falschen Sätze.

	(✔)	(✘)
1. I have got a good mark in my test. There weren't much mistakes in my test.	☐	☐
2. Our garage isn't very big. There's only space for one bike.	☐	☐
3. Oh, we haven't got enough milk. There's not much left in the bottle.	☐	☐
4. We can bake a cake, but there aren't many eggs for it in the fridge.	☐	☐
5. I'm so thirsty. Can I have milk, please?	☐	☐

a) ______

b) ______

5 Was würdest du auf Englisch sagen, wenn…

1. … du siehst, dass fünf Dosen Hundefutter im Schrank sind.

There are ______

2. … du drei Riegel Schokolade in einer Minute essen kannst.

I can ______

3. … du vier Tüten Chips für deinen Geburtstag brauchst.

I need ______

1 Schreibe die Zahlwörter in Ziffern auf.

1. The German football team won the world championship in ________ (nineteen hundred and fifty-four), ________ (nineteen hundred and seventy-four) and in ________ (nineteen ninety).
2. The biggest football stadium is in Barcelona in Spain. ____________ (ninety-eight thousand and eight hundred) people can watch a game there.
3. More than ____________________ (two hundred and fifty million) people play football today.

2 Manche Zahlen haben im Englischen schwierige oder besondere Schreibweisen. Schreibe die folgenden Zahlen als Wörter auf.

a) die Zweite ____________________ b) 12 ____________________

c) 13 ____________________ d) 23 ____________________

e) der 20ste ____________________ f) der 31ste ____________________

g) 40 ____________________ h) 1,000,000,000 ____________________

i) 400,000 ____________________ j) 101 ____________________

____________________ ____________________

3 Setze some oder any ein.

1. Mum, I need ________ new T-shirts. I can't find ________ nice T-shirts in my wardrobe.
2. Would you buy me ________ new white T-shirts, please?
3. I can't buy you ________ more T-shirts. I bought you ________ last weekend.
4. But I haven't got ________ good white T-shirts. I need ________ for my new jeans.
5. You don't need ________ new white T-shirts. You can wear one of your sister's T-shirts.
6. But Sarah has only got ________ old white T-shirts. They're nearly grey. I don't like them.

Test 3

4 Setze das richtige Wort ein.

1. Joe can see ______________ (jemanden) in the garden. But I can't see ______________ (niemanden).
2. There is ______________ (nichts) to do. I prepared ______________ (alles) yesterday.
3. Did you forget ______________ (irgendetwas)? No, ______________ (nichts).
4. Let's go ______________ (irgendwohin). We can go ______________ (irgendwohin).
5. ______________ (jeder) knows Berlin. ______________ (niemand) knows my little home town.

5 Eine Party steht ins Haus. Übersetze die Sätze. Die Wörter in den Boxen helfen dir.

organise invite listen to invite need	everything anybody somewhere nobody everybody

1. Ich möchte alle einladen. *I want to* ______________
2. Papa möchte niemanden einladen. *Dad* ______________
3. Meine Schwester möchte alles organisieren. *My sister* ______________
4. Wir brauchen irgendwo einen Partyraum. *We* ______________
5. Niemand will Oldies hören. ______________ *oldies.*

6 Übersetze die Mengenangaben.

1. etwas Zucker: ______________
2. wenig Zucker: ______________
3. viel Zucker: ______________
4. kein Zucker: ______________
5. 1 Päckchen Zucker: ______________
6. 1 Pfund Zucker: ______________

7 Welches Wort passt nicht in die Reihe, weil es zählbar ist? Schreibe es auf.

1. flour, sugar, eggs, water ______________
2. butter, cake, tea, milk ______________

will-future

12

1

Lies dir die Texte in den Sprechblasen durch und ergänze die Regel. Überlege für jeden Satz, ob es sich um eine Vorhersage, eine Vermutung oder eine spontane Äußerung handelt.

1. Tomorrow, the weather will be warm and sunny.

2. I'm sure, Luke and Mike will come, too.

3. I hope we will meet some of our friends there.

4. I'm so tired. I'll go to bed early today.

Setze ein: *spontane Äußerungen, Vermutungen, Vorhersagen*

Das will-future benutzt man 1. für ______________________, besonders beim Wetter,

2. für ______________________, die mit I think, I hope oder I'm sure beginnen und

3. für ______________________ .

2

Bildung des will-future und Verneinung: Lies dir die Beispielsätze und die Regel durch und setze dann die richtigen Verbformen in die Sätze oder Fragen ein.

TIPP: Die Kurzform von will not ist won't.

Beispiel 1:	It will rain tomorrow.	It won't rain tomorrow.
Beispiel 2:	I hope Tim will talk to Tina.	I hope Tim won't talk to Tina.

Das will-future wird für alle Personen im Singular und im Plural mit will + Grundform gebildet.
Die Verneinung wird für alle Personen im Singular und Plural mit won't + Grundform gebildet.

won't be — will win — won't rain — will make — will start

1. Look at the blue sky. It ______________________ this afternoon.
2. I'm hungry. – OK, I ______________________ you a big sandwich.
3. I think the party ______________________ at 3 o'clock.
4. Tim is sure that he ______________________ the competition.
5. You can leave your jacket at home. It ______________________ cold.

will-future

3 Lies den Wetterbericht und unterstreiche alle will-future Formen. Es sind elf. Zeichne dann den Wetterbericht mit Hilfe der vorgegebenen Symbole in die Karte ein.

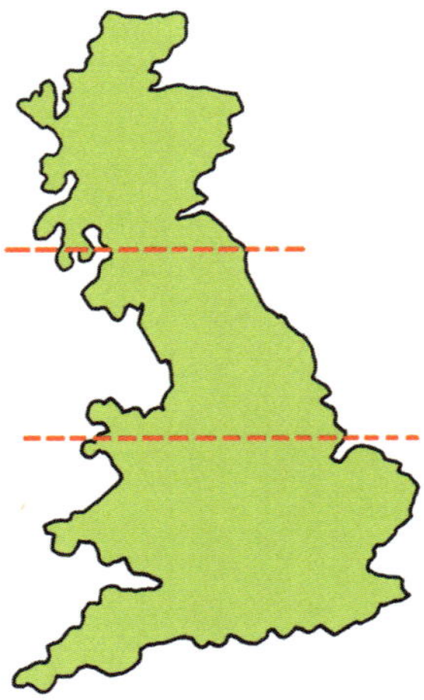

Good evening, ladies and gentlemen. Tomorrow we will have a warm and sunny day. There will be sunshine in the south all day. We'll have sunshine and a few clouds in the middle of the country, but it will stay warm and it won't rain. It'll be windy in the north and there will be some rain in the afternoon. Well, what will the temperatures be like? We'll have about 20 degrees in the south and in the middle. Only in the north there will be 15-18 degrees. The weather will stay warm and friendly for the whole week.

4 Bilde die entsprechenden bejahten oder verneinten Sätze.

1. I'm sure she will forget it.	I'm sure she ______
2. It ______	It won't rain in the afternoon.
3. I think they'll write a test tomorrow.	I'm sure they ______
4. Paul will take the train to London.	Paul ______
5. There ______	There won't be a storm tonight.

5 Ordne die Satzteile zu einem vollständigen Satz.

1. first | I'm sure | I'll be | race | in the ______
2. vegetables | again / won't eat | Maria ______
3. very | It'll rain | and | cold | it'll be ______
4. on Sunday | restaurants | won't be | The | open ______

if-Sätze Typ I

1 Verbinde die Satzteile sinnvoll miteinander.

1. If it is hot at the weekend,	a) I'll watch the film at home.
2. If Susan goes to the birthday party,	b) I'll go shopping with you.
3. If our English teacher is ill tomorrow,	c) she will bring a nice present.
4. If we get our new TV tomorrow,	d) we'll go to the swimming pool.
5. If I finish my homework early this afternoon,	e) we won't write the test.

If-Sätze bestehen immer aus einem Nebensatz, dem if-Satz, und einem Hauptsatz.
Der if-Satz kann am Satzanfang oder am Satzende stehen.
Im if-Satz steht das simple present, im Hauptsatz steht das will-future.

2 Vergleiche die beiden englischen Sätze und achte auf die Zeiten in der deutschen Übersetzung.

If it rains, I'll stay at home.	Wenn es regnet, bleibe ich zu Hause.
I'll stay at home if it rains.	Ich bleibe zu Hause, wenn es regnet.

Steht der if-Satz vorne, wird er mit einem Komma vom Hauptsatz abgetrennt, steht der if-Satz hinten, entfällt das Komma.

Im Deutschen können wir Zukünftiges mit der Gegenwart ausdrücken. Daher darf im Deutschen in beiden Satzteilen die Gegenwart stehen.
Im Englischen dagegen folgt auf einen if-Satz mit simple present ein Hauptsatz im will-future!

Übersetze nun diese beiden Sätze:

1. If it snows, I'll wear my new boots. ______________________

2. I'll watch the film here if that's ok. ______________________

3 If-Sätze mit Verneinung. Verbinde sie mit der richtigen deutschen Übersetzung.

1. If you <u>don't come</u> to the party, I'll be sad.	a) Ich bin nicht traurig, wenn du später kommst.
2. I <u>won't be</u> sad if you come later.	b) Ich bin nicht glücklich, wenn du nicht kommst.
3. I <u>won't be</u> happy, if you <u>don't come</u>.	c) Wenn du nicht zur Party kommst, bin ich traurig.

if-Sätze Typ I

TIPP

Im if-Satz brauchst du zur Verneinung das Hilfsverb do. Im Hauptsatz wird natürlich das Hilfsverb will verneint. Aber auch wenn die Verben verneint werden ändert das nichts an der Regel für die unterschiedlichen Zeiten in beiden Satzteilen.

4 Setze das Verb in der richtigen Zeit ein.

1. If you run quicker, you ______________________ (*catch*) the bus.
2. If you ______________________ (*not be*) careful with the water kettle, you will burn your hand.
3. If you eat too much chocolate, you ______________________ (*feel*) sick.
4. If you don't dry your long hair after swimming, you ________________ (*get*) a cold.

5 Du weißt schon, dass der *if*-Satz nicht immer vorne stehen muss. Die Regel für die Zeiten in *if*-Sätzen ändert sich dadurch nicht. Setze auch hier die Verben in der richtigen Zeit ein.

1. If you ______________________ (*not learn*) for your vocabulary test, you won't write a good test.
2. I ______________________ (*call*) Tina this afternoon if you give me her telephone number.
3. I'll make a cake for Grandma if she ______________________ (*come*) tomorrow.
4. If it is cold and windy, we ______________________ (*not play*) outside.

6 In der folgenden Übung musst du jeweils zwei Verben in der richtigen Zeit einsetzen.

1. If it ______________ (*be*) nice and warm outside, we ______________ (*drive*) to an amusement park.
2. You ____________ (*not get*) into the house if you ____________ (*lose*) your key.
3. If I ____________ (*find*) my wallet, I ____________ (*be*) happy.
4. I ____________ (*call*) you if you ____________ (*want*).

1 Übersetze die folgenden spontanen Äußerungen. Die Verben unten helfen dir.

help wait buy hurt call

1. Warte eine Moment. Ich helfe dir.

____

2. Keine Milch? Ich kaufe zwei Flaschen im Supermarkt.

____

3. Mein Bein tut weh. OK, ich rufe den Arzt an.

____

2 Trage die richtigen Verbformen für die Wettersätze ein.

This afternoon it (1) ______________ (*be*) nice with some clouds in the west. But it (2) ______________ (*rain*) in the evening and it (3) ______________ (*not stop*) until the early morning hours. Tomorrow the weather (4) ______________ (*start*) friendly. In the afternoon you (5) ______________ (*see*) some clouds again, but it (6) ______________ (*not rain*). The wind (7) ______________ (*come*) from the west. Temperatures at night (8) ______________ (*be*) around 10 degrees all over the country. It (9) ______________ (*become*) warmer tomorrow, we (10) ______________ (*have*) temperatures of 18 degrees in the north and 22 degrees in the south.

3 Übersetze ins Deutsche.

1. I'm sure, Mum will prepare a party for my birthday.

____

2. I think I'll buy her some flowers.

____

3. I hope we won't get any homework tomorrow.

____

Test 4

4 Setz die Verben in der richtigen Zeit ein.

1. If you ____________ (*bake*) the cake, I ____________ (*make*) the salad.
2. If we ____________ (*invite*) Laura, we ____________ (*have*) a lot of fun.
3. If we ____________ (*not buy*) coke, Tim ____________ (*be*) sad.
4. If Maya ____________ (*not come*), we ____________ (*not have*) any good CDs.

5 Was könntest du vorhaben, wenn …

(1) build a snowman
(2) write a bad mark
(3) go to the cinema more often
(4) be very happy

1. … es morgen schneit?

If it snows tomorrow, ____________

2. … ihr morgen einen Englischtest schreibt?

If we ____________

____

3. … deine Eltern dir mehr Taschengeld geben?

If my parents ____________

____

4. … Mark deine Hausaufgaben für dich macht?

If Mark ____________

____

6 Übersetze ins Deutsche.

1. I'll bake you a cake if you want.

____

2. My sister won't play in the band if she doesn't feel better.

____

3. Mum's friend will cut your hair if you ask her nicely.

____

Present perfect

1

Verbinde die englischen mit den deutschen Aussagen.
Unterstreiche die Signalwörter.

1. I have never been to Africa.
2. Sina has already been to Africa.
3. I've been in Africa for two years.
4. I haven't been to Africa yet.
5. Sina has just been to Africa.
6. I have been in Africa since 2005.

a) Sina war schon mal in Afrika.
b) Ich bin seit 2005 in Afrika.
c) Ich war noch nie in Afrika.
d) Ich war (bis jetzt) noch nicht in Afrika.
e) Ich bin schon zwei Jahre lang in Afrika.
f) Sina war gerade in Afrika.

Das present perfect wird immer mit have / has oder haven't / hasn' t + 3. Form des Verbs, dem past participle gebildet. Bei regelmäßigen Verben wird das past participle wie im simple past mit –ed gebildet. Bei unregelmäßigen Verben ist die Form ganz anders und du musst sie einfach lernen (auch wie im simple past). Auf S. 117 findest du eine Liste aller unregelmäßigen Verben.
Das present perfect wird gebraucht für Handlungen und Ereignisse, die sich in der Vergangenheit abspielen und noch in der Gegenwart von Bedeutung sind.
Signalwörter für *perfect*-Formen sind yet, not yet, already, just, ever, never sowie for und since.

2

Übersetze die beiden Sätze mit for und since.

1. We have lived in Berlin **for** 10 years.

____

2. We have lived in Berlin **since** 2000.

____

Zeitangaben im present perfect können mit for oder since gebildet werden. Beide Wörter entsprechen dem deutschen Wort **seit.** Wenn es um einen Zeit**raum** geht, benutzt man im Englischen for (z.B. for two weeks, for years, for five hours*)*. Wird ein genauer Zeit**punkt** angegeben, benutzt man since (z.B. since yesterday, since last Sunday, since 1995).

In bejahten Aussagen und Fragen im present perfect benutzt man das Wort already in der Bedeutung **schon.**
In verneinten Aussagen und Fragen im present perfect benutzt man das Wort yet. Es bedeutet dann in Fragen **schon** und in verneinten Aussagen **noch nicht.**

Present perfect

3 Nico bekommt jedes Wochenende eine Liste mit Dingen, die er zu erledigen hat. Schreibe auf, was Nico schon gemacht hat ✔, und was er noch nicht erledigt hat ✘.

1. *Nico has already fed the cat.*
2. ______
3. ______
4. ______
5. ______
6. ______

7. ______
8. ______

4 Übersetze die Sätze. Lass dich nicht vom Deutschen verleiten, eine bestimmte Zeit zu benutzen. Denke immer an die Signalwörter!

1. Ich bin noch nie in Großbritannien gewesen.

______

2. Wir haben uns gestern einen Hund gekauft.

______

3. Wir sind gerade aus Berlin zurückgekommen.

______

TIPP

be – was / were – been
buy – bought – bought
come – came – come
feed – fed – fed
learn – learnt – learnt
put – put – put
take – took – taken
think – thought – thought

Present perfect: **Fragen und Kurzantworten**

1 Jessica and Jane's afternoon

Unterstreiche die Perfektformen in jeder Sprechblase.

2 Übersetze, was Jessica und Jane sagen und fülle die Lücken aus.

Jessica: Hi Jane, ________ du deine Hausaufgaben ________ ________ ?

Jane: Nein. Aber ich ________ die Englischübungen ________ ________ .

Jessica: Klasse! ________ du schon ________ , wohin wir heute Abend gehen sollen?

Jane: Ja. Ich ________ gerade zwei Karten für den neuen Film im CINEMOVIE ________ .

Fragen im present perfect werden gebildet, indem man have oder has mit dem Subjekt vertauscht und an den Satzanfang stellt. Bei Kurzantworten wird nur have oder has wieder aufgegriffen.

3

Hier sind einige typische present perfect Fragen. Jeder der drei englischen Frageanfänge hat zwei deutsche Bedeutungen. Verbinde die Frageanfänge mit den beiden deutschen Bedeutungen, die passen. Ergänze dann die Regel.

1. Have you **ever** ...?
2. Have you **never** ...?
3. Have you **already**...?

a) Hast du **schon**...? Hast du **schon mal**...?
b) Hast du **jemals**...? Hast du **je**...?
c) Hast du **nie**...? Hast du **noch nie**...? Hast du **niemals**...?
d) Bist du **schon**...? Bist du **schon mal**...?
e) Bist du **jemals**...? Bist du **je**...?
f) Bist du **nie**...? Bist du **noch nie**...? Bist du **niemals**...?

Setze ein: *sein, haben, hat, habe, bin, ist, seid, habt*

Im Deutschen werden manche Perfektformen mit ________ (z.B. ich ________ gegessen, er ________ gegessen, ihr ________ gegessen) und manche Perfektformen mit ________ (z.B. ich ________ geflogen, er ________ geflogen, ihr ________ geflogen) gebildet.

Im Englischen steht für jede Perfektform immer have / has + 3. Form!

Present perfect: **Fragen und Kurzantworten**

4 Beantworte die Fragen mit Kurzantworten.

1. Have you ever spoken to a real American? ____________________

2. Have you already read the English book? ____________________

3. Has your best friend ever forgotten your birthday? ____________________

4. Have your neighbours ever had a cat? ____________________

5 Unterstreiche die Signalwörter für das present perfect und übersetze die Fragen und Antworten.

1a. Have you already bought a present for your Mum's birthday?

____

____

1b. No, I haven't had a good idea yet.

____

2a. Have you ever been to Berlin?

____

2b. Yes, I have. I've already spent a whole week there.

____

____

3a. Have you ever flown in a helicopter?

____

3b. No, I've never flown in a helicopter or a plane.

____

____

TIPP

flow – flew – flown
read – read – read

be – was / were – been
forget – forgot – forgotten
speak – spoke – spoken

buy – bought – bought
have – had – had
spend – spent – spent

Im Vergleich: *simple past* und *present perfect*

16

1 Unterstreiche bei den folgenden Sätzen die Signalwörter für das simple past rot und die Signalwörter für das present perfect grün.

1. Dad sold our car last Friday.
2. We haven't eaten pizza for two weeks.
3. I haven't called the doctor yet.
4. Three years ago my sister went to the USA.
5. They built the church in 1888.
6. Nobody has seen the cat since Wednesday.
7. Have you ever seen a famous sports star?
8. I've just spoken to your English teacher.
9. Nick had an accident an hour ago.
10. I went shopping with Rebecca yesterday.

TIPP

build – built – built	eat – ate – eaten
go – went - gone	see – saw – seen
sell – sold – sold	speak – spoke – spoken

2 Trage die Signalwörter aus Übung 1 in die Tabelle ein.

Signalwörter für das simple past	Signalwörter für das present perfect
1. ______	2. ______
3. ______	4. ______
5. ______	6. ______
7. ______	8. ______
9. ______	10. ______

3 Übersetze die Signalwörter aus Übung 2.

1. ______ 3. ______

3. ______ 5. ______

5. ______ 7. ______

7. ______ 9. ______

9. ______ 10. ______

Im Vergleich: *simple past* und *present perfect*

4 Setze simple past oder present perfect ein. Achte auf die Signalwörter.

1. I ______________ (*miss*) the bus this morning, so I ______________ (*be*) late for school.
2. Nina ______________ (*not be*) to school for 5 days. She ______________ (*break*) her leg last weekend.
3. ______________ you ______________ (*clean*) your shoes yet? Yes, I ______________ (*clean*) them right after school.
4. I ______________ (*finish*) my German homework at 5 o'clock. ______________ you already ______________ (*finish*) your homework?
5. Our neighbours ______________ (*book*) their holiday last Saturday, but we ______________________ (*not book*) our holiday yet.

5 Schreibe verneinte Aussagen im simple past und im present perfect.

1. Max has finished his homework. *Max hasn't finished his homework yet.*
2. I went to New York last summer. ______________________________
3. The train arrived at 8 o'clock. ______________________________
4. I've just called the doctor. ______________________________

6 Stelle Martin ein paar Fragen. Benutze simple past oder present perfect.

1. Frage ihn, ob er letzte Nacht gut geschlafen hat.

____

2. Frage ihn, ob ihm Jims Party am Wochenende gefallen hat.

____

3. Frage ihn, ob er jemals in einem amusement park war.

____

4. Frage ihn, ob er schon mal in Deutschland Sauerkraut gegessen hat.

____

Unregelmäßige Verben

1 Welche Verben sind regelmäßig, welche sind unregelmäßig?
Schreibe alle drei Formen auf.

work wake walk arrive ride read

bark make help sleep

TIPP: Wenn du bei den unregelmäßigen Verben die 3. Form noch nicht kennst, kannst du sie im Anhang auf S. 117 nachschlagen.

Regelmäßige Verben: 1. ______ 2. ______

3. ______ 4. ______ 5. ______

Unregelmäßige Verben:

Grundform (1.Form)	simple past form (2.Form)	past participle form (3.Form)
6. ______	______	______
7. ______	______	______
8. ______	______	______
9. ______	______	______
10. ______	______	______

Regelmäßige Verben haben in der 2. und der 3. Form die Endung –ed! Unregelmäßige Verben haben ganz unterschiedliche 2. und 3. Formen. Man muss sie einfach lernen.

2 Die Farbpatrone des Computers ist bald leer. Einige Buchstaben druckt er schon nicht mehr. Ergänze die Lücken. Jeder Kasten steht für einen Buchstaben.

1. gew□nnen: w□n – w□n – won
2. verl□□ren: l□se – l□st – lost
3. z□□chnen: draw – dr□w – dr□wn
4. fli□□en: fl□ – fl□w – fl□wn
5. spr□chen: sp□□k – spoke – sp□ken
6. re□□en: run – r□n – run
7. b□deuten: m□□n – m□□nt – meant
8. verl□tzen, wehtun: h□rt – hurt – h□rt
9. tr□nk□n: dr□nk – dr□nk – dr□nk
10. n□□men: t□ke – t□□k – t□k□n

Unregelmäßige Verben

3 Manche unregelmäßigen Verben kannst du auch paarweise lernen, weil sich ihre 2. und 3. Formen jeweils reimen. Sprich sie beim Lernen laut aus, dann prägen sich die Formen leichter ein.

1. tell und sell	2. keep und sleep	3. send und spend	4. cut und shut
5. teach und catch	6. fight und think	7. know und throw	8. take und shake

Schreibe die Paare nun mit ihren drei Formen auf.

1. *tell – told – told* wie *sell – sold – sold*
2. ______ wie ______
3. ______ wie ______
4. ______ wie ______
5. ______ wie ______
6. ______ wie ______
7. ______ wie ______
8. ______ wie ______

4 Warum muss man die unregelmäßigen Verben eigentlich lernen?

Du weißt schon, dass die 2. und 3. Form zur Bildung von unterschiedlichen Zeiten gebraucht wird. Du musst besonders die unregelmäßigen Verben lernen, damit du in englischen Texten erkennst, um welches Verb es sich handelt.

Erkennst du die Grundformen der folgenden past participle-Formen? Schreibe sie auf.

1. swum kommt von ______
2. gone kommt von ______
3. left kommt von ______
4. met kommt von ______
5. chosen kommt von ______
6. done kommt von ______
7. been kommt von ______
8. eaten kommt von ______

Unregelmäßige Verben

5 Merke dir diese sechs Verben mit einer außergewöhnlichen 2. und 3. Form.
Schreibe alle drei Formen auf und ordne die deutsche Übersetzung zu.

fangen unterrichten kaufen bringen kämpfen denken

Grundform	2. Form (simple past)	3. Form (past participle)	Übersetzung
1. catch	_____	_____	_____
2. teach	_____	_____	_____
3. buy	_____	_____	_____
4. bring	_____	_____	_____
5. fight	_____	_____	_____
6. think	_____	_____	_____

Der erste gesprochene Buchstabe bleibt in allen drei Formen gleich.
Die 2. und 3. Form ist bei allen sechs Verben gleich.
Zwei Verben haben in der 2. und 3. ein aught (teach und catch), die anderen 4 haben ein ought. Die Endungen werden alle gleich ausgesprochen: sie reimen sich!

6 Auch wer die deutsche Sprache lernt, muss bei den deutschen Verben drei Formen lernen, die für unterschiedliche Zeiten benutzt werden.
Schreibe die englischen Entsprechungen.

1. fahren – fuhr – gefahren: *drive – drove – driven*
2. schließen – schloss – geschlossen: _____
3. haben – hatte – gehabt: _____
4. verstehen – verstand – verstanden: _____
5. bringen – brachte – gebracht: _____
6. riechen – roch – gerochen: _____

Unregelmäßige Verben

7 Im Wortgitter sind fünf **Grundformen**, fünf **simple past-Formen** und fünf **past participle-Formen** waagerecht versteckt. Finde sie, ordne sie der Tabelle zu und ergänze die fehlenden Formen.

S	D	O	N	E	P	O	S	A	W	Z	E	W	A
F	E	E	L	J	K	M	O	F	V	W	O	R	N
P	U	R	E	T	H	R	O	W	F	W	A	S	E
E	A	S	A	Y	B	R	O	K	T	A	K	E	N
G	I	M	N	T	E	A	C	H	K	E	R	T	S
O	S	H	O	W	N	G	A	T	E	N	G	E	T
B	E	C	A	M	E	H	O	L	P	E	R	N	T
F	A	K	N	E	W	L	E	D	R	I	V	E	N

Grundform	simple past Form	past participle Form
1. ______	______	______
2. ______	______	______
3. ______	______	______
4. ______	______	______
5. ______	______	______
______	6. ______	______
______	7. ______	______
______	8. ______	______
______	9. ______	______
______	10. ______	______
do	did	11. done
______	______	12. ______
______	______	13. ______
______	______	14. ______
______	______	15. ______

1 Übersetze die folgenden Fragen und Sätze. Denke an die Signalwörter und lass dich nicht von den Zeiten im Deutschen in die Irre führen!

1. Hast du schon zu Mittag gegessen?

___

2. Mein Bruder hat mein Fahrrad noch nicht repariert.

___

3. Warst du schon mal in Paris?

___

4. Ich bin noch nie in einem Museum gewesen.

___

5. Ich habe gerade deine neuen Jeans gewaschen.

___

6. Habt ihr schon mal ein Haustier gehabt?

___

2 Vervollständige die Kurzantworten.

1. Have you ever been to a pop concert? Yes, ___
2. Have you ever seen a real snake? No, ___
3. Have you already slept in a youth hostel? Yes, ___
4. Have your parents ever gone on holiday without you? No, ___
5. Has your best friend ever bought the same T-shirt as you? Yes, ___
6. Have you ever been to hospital? No, ___
7. Has your English teacher ever forgotten his English book? No, ___
8. Have you and your friend ever played a trick on somebody? Yes, ___

Test 5

3 Setze die Verben in der richtigen Zeit ein.

1. ________________ you ________________ (*check*) the e-mails? Yes, I ________________ (*check*) them ten minutes ago. But I ________________ (*not get*) your e-mail yet.
2. Maya ____________ (stay) in bed for three days. She's feeling much better now.
3. Dad ________________ (*buy*) a new camera yesterday. He ________________ (*look*) for a cheap one since last summer.
4. Hi, Julian. I ________________ just ________________ (*finish*) my homework. ________________ you ________________ yet?
5. I know everything. I ________________ just ________________ (*speak*) to your dad.
6. Our neighbours want to move to Bonn. They ________________ (*live*) here for 5 years.

4 Ordne die folgenden Zeitformen in der Tabelle den richtigen Zeiten zu.

haven't taken · has broken · felt · didn't make · understood · didn't forget · has phoned · hasn't eaten

simple past	present perfect
________________	________________
________________	________________
________________	________________
________________	________________

5 Wie heißen die drei Formen folgender unregelmäßigen Verben?

1. write ____________ ____________
2. read ____________ ____________
3. pay ____________ ____________
4. have ____________ ____________
5. feel ____________ ____________
6. find ____________ ____________
7. tell ____________ ____________
8. do ____________ ____________
9. be ____________ ____________
10. teach ____________ ____________

would, could, Would you like ...?

18

1 Verbinde die passenden Paare miteinander.

1. What would **you** do?
2. Can I go to the cinema?
3. Would you help me, please?
4. Could you open the door, please?
5. Can I help you?
6. Would you like a drink?
7. Could I have some sugar, please?
8. Could you say that again, please?
9. What would you like?

a) Kann ich ins Kino gehen?
b) Was würdest **du** tun?
c) Was hättest du gerne?
d) Können Sie das bitte noch einmal sagen?
e) Hättest du gerne ein Getränk?
f) Könnte ich bitte etwas Zucker haben?
g) Kann ich euch helfen?
h) Würdest du mir bitte helfen?
i) Könntest du bitte die Tür öffnen?

Can, would und could nennt man Modalverben (modal verbs). Sie werden besonders dann benutzt, wenn man **höflich** um etwas bitten möchte. Could ist dabei höflicher als can!

2 Was bedeuten would und could im Deutschen? Unterstreiche die deutschen Entsprechungen für die unterstrichenen Wörter.

1. What could we do?

   Was könnten wir tun?

2. We could go to the park and could eat an ice cream.

   Wir könnten in den Park gehen und könnten ein Eis essen.

3. What would you watch on TV, the love story or the talk show?

   Was würdest du im Fernsehen anschauen, die Liebesgeschichte oder die Talkshow?

4. I wouldn't watch the love story, I would watch the talk show.

   Ich würde mir nicht die Liebesgeschichte anschauen, ich würde die Talkshow anschauen.

5. Where could we stay?

   Wo könnten wir übernachten?

6. We could stay on a campsite. That would be great.

   Wir könnten auf einem Campingplatz übernachten. Das wäre großartig!

Would und could werden auch benutzt für Vorschläge oder Ansichten und Ereignisse, die eintreten können. Would und could stehen immer **mit dem Infinitiv** eines Verbs. Das ist übrigens im Deutschen auch so. Verneinungen heißen would not / wouldn't oder could not / couldn't.

would, could, Would you like ...?

3 Übersetze die Aussagen und Fragen ins Deutsche.

1. Would you buy this white T-shirt?

2. Could you close the window, please?

3. Grandma wouldn't want a computer.

4. We could phone Celine. She knows everything.

5. We could ask for a group ticket. That wouldn't be so expensive.

4 Übersetze ins Englische. Die Wörter im Kreis helfen dir.

go to the concert
ask Mum
pick us up
help
make a salad
bake a pizza
play tricks on us

1. Ich würde mit dir auf das Konzert gehen.

2. Wir könnten Mama fragen. Sie könnte uns abholen.

3. Könntest du Nicole bitte helfen?

4. Vera könnte einen Salat machen und ich könnte eine Pizza backen.

5. Joe würde mit uns keine Tricks machen.

Gerund als Subjekt und *gerund* als Objekt

19

1 Was ist ein gerund? Ergänze die Lücken in den deutschen und den englischen Sätzen. Unterstreiche alle englischen gerunds.

1. ______________ is my hobby, playing basketball is Lea's hobby.

   Fußballspielen ist mein Hobby, ______________ ist Leas Hobby.

2. Jogging in the park is fun, ______________ in the woods is more fun.

   ______________ im Park macht Spaß, Laufen im Wald macht mehr Spaß.

Setze ein: *Nomen, +ing, Artikel, verdoppelt, Verb be*

Gerunds werden aus Verben ______________ gebildet. Sie verwandeln sich damit zu ______________ (swim → swimming). Das geht auch im Deutschen (schwimmen → das Schwimmen). Manchmal muss man ein gerund im Deutschen umschreiben, z.B. ‚das Schreiben von Postkarten' oder ‚E-Mails zu schreiben' ...etc. Das gerund als Subjekt steht am Satzanfang. Ihm folgt meistens das ______________. Vor einem gerund steht im Englischen kein ______________! Beachte auch besondere Schreibweisen: Konsonanten am Wortende werden oft ______________, -e am Verbende fällt weg.

2 Manche Verben drücken eine Vorliebe (z.B. like) oder eine Abneigung (z.B. hate, don't like) aus. Nach solchen Verben folgt fast immer ein gerund. Bilde gerunds und ergänze die Sätze mit den vorgegebenen Satzteilen.

(1) play computer games
(2) repair bikes
(3) talk on the phone
(4) listen to music

1. I love ______________
2. My friends hate ______________
3. Mum likes ______________
4. My parents don't like ______________

Setze ein: *Abneigung, Objekt, Vorliebe*

Ein gerund kann auch ______________ in einem Satz sein. Dabei steht es vor allem nach Verben, die eine ______________ (like, love, enjoy) oder eine ______________ (*don't like, hate*) ausdrücken und nach einigen Sonderfällen (u.a. How about...?)

Gerund als Subjekt und *gerund* als Objekt

3 Bringe die Satzteile in die richtige Reihenfolge.

1. cinema | going | to the | activity | favourite | is my

2. interested in | cards | I'm | collecting | football | very

3. I | on Saturdays | TV | love | in bed | watching

4 Übersetze ins Englische und benutze dabei ein gerund.

1. Meine Hobbys sind Schwimmen und Tennisspielen.

2. Klavierspielen ist manchmal langweilig.

3. Martha und John genießen es Ferien zu haben.

4. Was können wir tun? – Wie wär's mit Kartenspielen?

5. Ich interessiere mich nicht fürs Tanzen. Ich kann Tanzen nicht ausstehen.

TIPP

„Ich kann das nicht ausstehen." heißt im Englischen: I can't stand that.
Nach can't stand kommt in der Regel ein Nomen oder eben auch ein gerund:
I can't stand cleaning my shoes.

1 Übersetze das Gespräch am Frühstückstisch. Sei höflich und benutze Would you…, Would you like…, I would like…, Could I / you… und please. Die Wörter im Kasten helfen dir.

sit down here	spoon	muesli	toast after that	maybe	milk	cheese

Mum: Guten Morgen Mike. Würdest du dich bitte hierher setzen?

____

____

Mike: Guten Morgen. Könnte ich bitte einen Löffel haben? Ich würde gerne Müsli essen.

____

____

Mum: Hier, bitte. Möchtest du gerne ein Toast hinterher essen?

____

____

Mike: Ja, vielleicht. Könnte ich bitte die Milch haben?

____

____

Mum: Hättest du gerne Käse auf deinem Sandwich?

____

____

Mike: Ja, Käse ist OK. Danke.

____

2 Kannst du diese Sätze umschreiben, damit sie höflicher klingen? Benutze would / could.

1. What time is it? ______________________________
2. Where's the next bus station?

____

3. Show me the way. ______________________________

3 Bilde gerunds aus folgenden Verben. Achte dabei auf besondere Schreibweisen!

1. sit – ______________ 2. travel – ______________

3. run – ______________ 4. prepare – ______________

5. swim – ______________ 6. smile – ______________

7. dance – ______________ 8. leave – ______________

9. cut – ______________ 10. drive – ______________

4 Übersetze ins Deutsche.

1. How about bungee jumping? ______________
2. I can't stand cleaning football shoes. ______________

____
3. Mum enjoys cooking very much. ______________
4. Travelling is really great. ______________

5 Was mögen diese Jungen und Mädchen und was mögen sie nicht? Übersetze die Sprechblasen und benutze ein gerund. Denke an die korrekte Satzstellung im Englischen: S-V-O!

Jack: Ich hasse Fahrräder zu reparieren.

Lucy: Ich liebe es lange Briefe zu schreiben.

Ron: Ich genieße es am Wochenende viel zu schlafen.

Chiara: Ich mag Vokabellernen nicht.

Julie: Ich interessiere mich fürs Zeichnen.

Mario: Ich kann Fußballspielen nicht ausstehen.

1. **Jack:** ______________
2. **Lucy:** ______________
3. **Chiara:** ______________
4. **Ron:** ______________
5. **Julie:** ______________
6. **Mario:** ______________

to be able to, to be allowed to, to have to

20

1 Du kennst schon einige modals (Modalverben). Übersetze sie.

I can speak English.
Tom could speak English.

can - ______________

You may eat the biscuits.
Peter may go to the cinema.

may - ______________

Tim must be at home at six.
Barbara must look good tomorrow.

must - ______________

Für jedes dieser modals gibt es eine Ersatzform. Sie lautet:
can → Ersatzform: **to be able to**
may → Ersatzform: **to be allowed to**
must → Ersatzform: **to have to**

2 Modals sind besondere Verben. Schau dir die Beispielsätze oben genau an und kreuze dann bei den folgenden Aussagen an, was auf die modals can, may und must zutrifft.

1. ☐ Die modals can, may und must können nie alleine stehen, ihnen folgt immer ein Infinitiv ohne to.
2. ☐ Die modals may und must kommen bis auf can nur im simple present vor.
3. ☐ Die modals can, may und must haben im simple present in der 3. Person Singular kein -s!
4. ☐ Die modals can, may und must haben für alle andere Zeiten als das simple present eine Ersatzform.
5. ☐ Die Ersatzformen für modals werden alle mit be oder mit have gebildet.
6. ☐ Im simple present kann man das modal **oder** seine Ersatzform benutzen.

3 Modals und Ersatzformen in unterschiedlichen Zeiten:

simple present	simple past	will-future
can / am, are, is able to	could / was, were able to	will be able to
may / am, are, is allowed to	was, were allowed to	will be allowed to
must / have, has to	had to	will have to

Wenn du die Formen von be und have in allen Zeiten kannst, dann hast du keine Probleme mit den Ersatzformen der modals. Denn nur be oder have müssen in die entsprechende Zeit versetzt werden, der Rest der Ersatzform bleibt unverändert.

to be able to, to be allowed to, to have to

4 Hier siehst du Ersatzformen von modals in verschiedenen Zeiten, auch in verneinten Formen. Bestimme die Zeitform und schreibe das dazugehörige modal daneben.

Ersatzform in verschiedenen Zeiten	Welche Zeit ist es?	Von welchem *modal* ist es die Ersatzform?
1. (I) wasn't able to		
2. (you) have to		
3. (they) didn't have to		
4. (we) were allowed to		
5. (she) doesn't have to		
6. (I) wasn't allowed to		
7. (they) were able to		
8. (I) won't be allowed to		
9. (I) will be able to		
10. (he) will be allowed to		

5 Setze die folgenden Sätze ins simple past. Benutze eine Ersatzform.

1. I must do a lot of homework. ______________________ yesterday.
2. Bob may go to the cinema. ______________________ last Saturday.
3. Dad can repair Tina's bike. ______________________

6 Benutze die richtige Ersatzform und setze die folgenden Sätze ins will-future.

1. Mum can drive us to the concert. ______________________
2. You may go to the zoo. ______________________
3. My sister must phone her teacher. ______________________

Past progressive: Sätze mit while und when

21

1 Unterstreiche in jedem Haupt- und Nebensatz die Prädikate (Verben). Es sind acht.

At the football match last Saturday
While the two school teams were playing, it started to rain. Dave was running across the field when Max fell on the grass. While Max was holding his left leg, the trainer called the ambulance. When the ambulance came, a lot of players were standing around Max.

In jedem Satz hast du ein Verb im simple past und ein Verb im past progressive gefunden, stimmt's? Überprüfe noch einmal, ob das zutrifft.

Die Kombination von simple past und past progressive kommt sehr häufig vor. Sie wird benutzt, wenn man eine länger anhaltende Situation in der Vergangenheit beschreibt, in die ein kurzes Ereignis eintritt. Die länger anhaltende Situation steht im past progressive, das neu eintretende kürzere Ereignis steht im simple past.

2 Die Bildung des past progressive. Lies dir die Beispielsätze durch und ergänze die Erklärung.

They carried Max to the ambulance while the trainer **was talking** to the team. While the friends from school **were singing** and **clapping** their hands, Tom scored the second goal.

Setze ein: *wasn't / weren't, Verneinung, was / were, be, past progressive*

Das ______________________ wird mit einer Form von ______ im simple past (______________________) + ing-Form gebildet. Die ______________________ im past progressive wird mit ______________________ + ing-Form gebildet.

3 While und when: Lies die Sätze und ergänze die Regel

While Dave was trying to score a third goal, the referee stopped the game.
When the teams left the field, the fans were still singing.

Setze ein: *simple past* (2x), *past progressive* (2x)
While und when leiten Nebensätze ein, auf die ein Hauptsatz folgt. Dabei gelten für beide Konjunktionen unterschiedliche Regeln:

Im while-Satz steht das ______________, es folgt ein Haupsatz im ______________.

Im when-Satz steht das ______________, es folgt ein Hauptsatz mit ______________.

Past progressive: **Sätze mit** *while* **und** *when*

4 Diese Geschichte von einem Fußballspiel kennst du schon, hier steht sie allerdings mit Lücken. Fülle sie mit den richtigen Verbformen aus.

While the two school teams (1) ____________________ (*play*), it (2) ____________________ (*start*) to rain. Dave (3) ____________________ (*run*) across the field when Max (4) ____________________ (*fall*) on the grass. While Max (5) ____________________ (*hold*) his left leg, the trainer (6) ____________________ (*call*) the ambulance. When the ambulance (7) ____________________ (*come*), a lot of players (8) ____________________ (*stand*) around Max. They (9) ____________________ (*carry*) Max to the ambulance while the trainer (10) ____________________ (*talk*) to the team. While the friends from school (11) ____________________ (*sing*) and (12) ____________________ (*clap*) their hands, Tom (13) ____________________ (*score*) the second goal. While Dave (14) ____________________ (*try*) to score a third goal, the referee (15) ____________________ (*stop*) the game. When the teams (16) ____________________ (*leave*) the field, the fans (17) ____________________ (*still sing*).

TIPP

Das Wort still steht im progressive meistens zwischen dem Hilfsverb be und dem eigentlichen Verb.

5 Was taten die Kinder als ihre Englischlehrerin das Klassenzimmer betrat? Übersetze die deutschen Satzteile:

When Mrs Rolix entered the classroom, ...

1. ... ____________________
____________________ (aßen zwei Mädchen ihre Sandwiches)

2. ... ____________________
____________________ (saßen fünf Jungen auf dem Tisch)

3. ... ____________________
____________________ (stand ein Mädchen auf einem Stuhl)

4. ... ____________________ (lachten zwei Mädchen)

5. ... ____________________ (warf ein Junge einen Ball)

1 Setze eine passende Ersatzform in der richtigen Zeit in die Sätze.

have to · have to · be allowed to · have to · be able to · not be allowed to

1. Lily ______________________ go to Kim's birthday party last Friday.
2. Laura ______________________ look in five different shops for a nice T-shirt until she found one.
3. After three years I ______________________ speak English quite well.
4. After the school party we ______________________ do all the cleaning. That was hard work.
5. Tomorrow I ______________________ look after my sister. My parents will go out.
6. The trip is too expensive. I'm sure we ______________________ come with you.

2 Übersetze diese kurzen Sätze. Benutze modals oder ihre Ersatzformen.

TIPP: auswendig lernen = to learn by heart

1. Ich kann das verstehen. ______________________
2. Ich konnte das nicht verstehen. ______________________
3. Ich werde das nicht verstehen können. ______________________
4. Du musst das auswendig lernen. ______________________
5. Wir mussten das auswendig lernen. ______________________
6. Ihr werdet das auswendig lernen müssen. ______________________
7. Ich durfte dich nicht anrufen. ______________________
8. Ihr dürft nach Hause gehen. ______________________

3 Verbinde die englischen Fragen mit den richtigen deutschen Fragen und ergänze dann die Lücken.

1. Will you be allowed to come?	a) Wirst du früh nach Hause gehen ____________?
2. Will you be able to prepare the food?	b) Wirst du kommen ____________?
3. Will you have to go home early?	c) Wirst du die Musik machen ____________?
4. Will you be allowed to make the music?	d) Wirst du das Essen vorbereiten ____________?

Test 7

4 Ergänze die Lücken mit der richtigen Form des Verbs.

When Susan and Helen arrived at the school party...

1. ... the school band ______________________ (*play*) rock music.
2. ... their best friends ______________________ (*stand*) in front of it.
3. ... some younger children ______________________ (*eat*) an ice-cream.
4. ... Mrs Rolix ______________________ (*talk*) to Marc's mother.
5. ... the head master ______________________ (*laugh*) with some parents.
6. ... Karen and Greg ______________________ (*sell*) cake.

5 Setze die richtigen Zeiten in die while- oder when-Sätze ein.

1. Mum ______________________ (*prepare*) my favourite meal when I ______________________ (*come*) home from school.
2. While I ______________________ (*do*) my homework in the evening, all the lights ______________________ (*go out*).
3. When we ______________________ (*land*) in London, it ______________________ (*rain*).
4. The pupils from year 7 ______________________ (*write*) a test when somebody ______________________ (*knock*) at the door.

6 Übersetze ins Englische. Diese Wörter helfen dir bei der Lösung.

shine
ring
on TV
mobile
arrive
football fans

1. Als ich aus dem Haus ging, schien die Sonne.

____

2. Während ich Fernsehen schaute, klingelte mein Handy.

____

3. Als wir am Bahnhof ankamen, sangen dort einen Menge Fußballfans.

____

____

1 Ordne den Inhalt der Sprechblasen den folgenden drei Kategorien zu.

What are you going to do this weekend?

I'm not going to do anything. I'm going to relax.

1. **Frage:** ______________________________

2. **Bejahte Aussage:** ______________________________

3. **Verneinte Aussage:** ______________________________

2 Schau dir noch einmal die Sätze aus Übung 1 genau an. Unterstreiche die Form von be rot. Unterstreiche das going to grün. Unterstreiche die Grundform des folgenden Verbs blau.

Du erkennst nun die Bausteine, die zur Bildung des going to futures nötig sind. Verändert wird je nach Person nur die Form von be und das Verb, das nach going to immer in der Grundform erscheint!

Das going to-future wird in bejahten und verneinten Aussagen so gebildet:
- eine Form von be + going to + Infinitiv des Verbs
- eine verneinte Form von be + going to + Infinitiv des Verbs

Bejahte Formen von be im simple present sind: am, are, is (kurz: 'm, 're, 's).
Verneinte Formen von be im simple present heißen: am not, are not, is not (kurz: 'm not, aren't, isn't)

3 Übersetze die Sprechblasen aus Übung 1.:

1. **Frage:** ______________________________

2. **Bejahte Aussage:** ______________________________

3. **Verneinte Aussage:** ______________________________

Das going to-future wird verwendet, wenn man einen **Plan** oder eine **Idee** für ein zukünftiges Ereignis hat. Es wird außerdem für **Vorhersagen** verwendet, wenn es **deutliche Anzeichen** für das tatsächliche Eintreten des Ereignisses gibt.
Denke daran, dass nicht jeder englische Satz im Futur im Deutschen auch mit Futur übersetzt werden muss. Im Deutschen verwenden wir oft die Gegenwart für Zukünftiges.

going to-future

4 Fülle die Lücken mit der richtigen Form im going to-future aus.

1. Grandma and Grandpa ______ (*visit*) us at the weekend.
2. They ______ (*stay*) until Monday.
3. Dad ______ (*cook*) his special dinner for all of us.
4. My sister and I ______ (*set*) the breakfast table on Sunday morning.
5. I ______ (*go*) for a walk with them and show them my school.

5 Benutze die folgenden Satzteile und bilde Fragen im going to-future.

1. you | bake | a cake | for your grandparents

______

2. you | tell | them | about | your last | English test

______

6 Übersetze Ninas Pläne und Ideen für die Schuldisko ins Deutsche.

1. I'm going to wear my new trousers and my new shoes. ______

______

2. I'm going to ask Sandra to bring her camera. ______

______

3. Tim will be the DJ. So we're going to listen to great music. ______

______

4. I'm not going to go home before ten o'clock. ______

______

Im Vergleich: *will-future* und *going to-future*

1 Lies die Sätze und Fragen aufmerksam durch. Unterstreiche die unterschiedlichen Futurformen und schreibe sie sortiert in die Tabelle.

1. I'm sure, Julia will meet Luca.
2. It's after eight! You're going to be late!
3. We hope it won't rain tomorrow.
4. We're going to go to France next summer.
5. I'm not going to tell you my marks.
6. It's so hot here. – I'll get you a drink.

will future	going to-future
will meet	*'re going to be*

Erinnerst du dich an die Regeln? Fülle die Lücken aus.

Das ____________ wird für alle Personen im Singular und im Plural mit will + **Grundform** gebildet.

Die Verneinung wird für alle Personen im Singular und Plural mit won't + **Grundform** gebildet. Das ____________ wird in bejahten und verneinten Aussagen so gebildet:
- eine Form von be + going to + **Infinitiv** des Verbs
- eine **verneinte** Form von be + going to + **Infinitiv** des Verbs

2 Vergleiche die Sätze und ergänze die Regel.

1. I'm sure, Julia will meet Luca.
2. It's after eight! You're going to be late!
3. The weather will be friendly tomorrow.
4. Look at the clouds. It's going to rain soon.

Setze ein: *spontane Äußerungen, Vorhersagen, Idee, Vermutungen, Plan*

Das will-future benutzt man 1. für ____________, besonders beim Wetter,

2. für ____________, die mit I think, I hope oder I'm sure beginnen und

3. für ____________. Das going to-future wird verwendet, wenn man einen ____________ oder eine ____________ für ein zukünftiges Ereignis hat. Es wird außerdem für Vorhersagen verwendet, wenn es deutliche Anzeichen für das tatsächliche Eintreten des Ereignisses gibt.

Im Vergleich: *will-future* und *going to-future*

3 Lies dir die folgenden Aussagen durch und entscheide, mit welcher Absicht etwas gesagt wurde. Kreuze deine Entscheidung in der Tabelle an.

1. Look at the dark sky! It's going to rain.
2. It won't rain at the weekend.
3. We're sure you'll be first in the race.
4. We're going to go to Berlin by train.
5. I'm going to play football with my friends.
6. I hope Tim will write a good test.
7. I've got no time! – I'll do the shopping for you.
8. There will be storms in the south.

	______________			______________	
Satz	**spontane Entscheidung**	**Wetter-vorhersage**	**Vermutungen mit *I'm sure, I think, I hope***	**Plan, Idee**	**Vorhersage mit deutlichen Anzeichen**
1.	○	○	○	○	○
2.	○	○	○	○	○
3.	○	○	○	○	○
4.	○	○	○	○	○
5.	○	○	○	○	○
6.	○	○	○	○	○
7.	○	○	○	○	○
8.	○	○	○	○	○

4 Schreibe nun in die zwei leeren Überschriftszeilen der Tabelle in Übung 3 die Wörter will-future und going to-future. Überprüfe deine Einträge und korrigiere sie, falls nötig.

5 Übersetze folgende Aussagen. (In Klammern steht ein Tipp für dich!)

1. Mama, da ist jemand an der Tür! – Warte, ich mach' die Tür auf. (*spontan*)

____

____

2. Wir werden eine großartige Party haben. (*Idee*)

____

3. Ich bin sicher, dass wir gewinnen. (*Vermutung*)

____

Possessivpronomen

1 Unterstreiche die Possessiv**begleiter** blau und die Possessiv**pronomen** grün.

1. This is my CD.
2. These are your neighbours.
3. Whose CDs are these? Are they yours?
4. This is her cat.
5. Whose exercise book is this? It's hers.
6. What about these shoes? They are mine.
7. This is their garden.
8. This is your friend.
9. This is his football.
10. These books? They're theirs.
11. They are all ours.
12. These are not yours.
13. Are those little balls over there its?
14. This is our house.
15. This is its food.
16. Whose lunch box is this? It's his.

2 Schreibe die Possessivpronomen und Possessivbegleiter an der richtigen Stelle in die Tabelle.

Personalpronomen	Possessivbegleiter	Possessivpronomen
I	my	mine
you		
he		
she		
it		
we		
you		
they		

Possessivpronomen stehen wie Personalpronomen für ein Substantiv (pro Nomen = für ein Nomen). Possessivpronomen können alleine stehen, verändern sich nicht und treten besonders häufig mit dem Verb be auf.

Possessivpronomen

3 Übersetze ins Englische.

1. Ist das mein Platz? Ja, das ist Ihrer.

Is this my seat? Yes its yours

2. Ich kann mein Buch nicht finden. Du kannst meins nehmen.

I cannot find my book. You can use mine

3. Wessen CDs sind dies? Das sind unsere, danke.

Whoose CD aretheese? Thats ours. thx

4 Fülle die Lücken aus. Personalpronomen, Possessivbegleiter und Possessivpronomen sind hier gefragt.

Anne: Pat, Gary, what are (1) you (*ihr*) doing?

Pat: We're looking for (2) our (*unsere*) coats. We're going in a minute.

Anne: But it's only 9 o'clock!

Pat: Yes, we have to take the 9.15 bus. It's the last one to Marx Street.

Gary: Where is (3) my (*mein*) coat? Pat, (4) yours (*deiner*) is over there but I can't find (5) mine (*meinen*).

Pat: Typical. It's five past nine and (6) you (*du*) can't find (7) your (*deinen*) coat.

Anne: Hey, listen. (8) We (*wir*) must find Gary's coat. Who can help (9) us (*uns*)?

Other kids: Is this one (10) yours (*deiner*)? – No, that is (11) mine (*meiner*)! And that one is (12) hers (*ihrer*). (13) His (*seiner*) is not here.

Pat: I'm going now. It's (14) your (*dein*) problem.

Gary: But (15) my (*mein*) coat! The bus! Oh no!

Anne: Hey, Gary, take (16) my (*meinen*) coat. It's big enough.

Gary: But it's a girl's coat.

Anne: So what? Look, (17) your (*dein*) bus is coming. Go on, hurry up.

1 Setze eine passende Form des Futurs in die Sätze ein.

'll get ~~'ll wait~~ 's going to 'll be 're going to won't come

1. **Tom:** I'm not yet ready. **Marvin:** Ok, I 'll wait for you.
2. Look at the dark clouds. It 's going to rain soon.
3. What are you going to do tomorrow? We 're going to go shopping.
4. Let's invite Tina to our party. I'm sure she 'll be happy.
5. What about Nick and Simon? I think they won't come.
6. Can I have a drink , please? Of course, I 'll get you a glass of water.

2 Mit welcher Begründung kannst du die Wahl deiner Futurformen in Übung 1 belegen? Setze ein Kreuzchen (✗).

Satz	spontane Entscheidung	Vermutung	Wetter-vorhersage	Plan, Idee	Vorhersage mit Anzeichen
1.					
2.					
3.					
4.					
5.					
6.					

3 Übersetze ins Englische.

1. Diese Taschen sind zu schwer. – Warte, ich helfe dir.

____

2. Am Wochenende wird es sonnig und trocken sein. Es wird nicht regnen.

____

____

4 Übersetze die Fragen ins Deutsche.

1. Are you going to walk to Lisa's house?

____

2. Is your brother going to buy that computer?

____

3. Are you and your friend going to do the project together?

____

5 Setze ein:

mine yours his hers ours yours theirs

1. Here are Finn's CDs.	They're not ________, they're Leo's.
2. Please bring back the Porters' plates.	Sorry, but they're not ________.
3. Tom, put your comics in your schoolbag.	They're not ________, Mrs Devon.
4. Please bring Angela's magazine upstairs.	That's not ________.
5. Maya and Linda, put your shoes away.	But Mum, they're not ________.
6. Look at these sweet little rabbits.	Are they ________?
7. There are three lunchboxes in the kitchen	The blue one is ________.

6 Übersetze ins Englische.

1. Das ist meins. ______________________________
2. Das sind nicht eure. ______________________________
3. Das sind jetzt ihre. 1. Möglichkeit: ______________________________
   2. Möglichkeit: ______________________________
4. Sind das eure? ______________________________
5. Ja, das sind unsere. ______________________________

Relativsätze mit Relativpronomen

25

1 Vergleiche die folgenden Sätze miteinander und ergänze die Regel.

1. This is the boy who / that told me everything about the football club. (Singular)
2. These are the children who / that always paint on the walls. (Plural)

3. This is the T-shirt which / that I bought yesterday. (Singular)
4. These are the books which / that I have to bring back to the library. (Plural)

Setze ein: *That, which, who,* Plural, Singular, Relativpronomen

Die ______________________ who, which und that lauten im ______________ und ______________ immer gleich, sie verändern sich nicht. ______________ bezieht sich aber nur auf Personen, ______________ nur auf Sachen. ______________ kann sowohl für Personen als auch für Sachen stehen.

2 Vergleiche nun die nächsten Sätze miteinander.

1. The boy who told me everything about the football club is very tall.
2. The children who always paint on the walls are still young.
3. The T-shirt which I bought yesterday was quite expensive.
4. The books which I have to bring back to the library are really heavy.

→ Relativpronomen Subjekt

5. I bought the T-shirt which I liked the most.
6. I didn't bring back the book which I haven't finished yet.
7. I like the boy who told me everything about the football club.
8. We saw the children who always paint on the walls.

→ Relativpronomen Objekt

Who, which oder that leiten Relativsätze ein, die sich auf das Subjekt oder auf das Objekt des Hauptsatzes beziehen können.

3 Das Relativpronomen whose.

This is the man whose dog always barks.

I'll show you a park whose trees are very old.

Whose wird für Personen **und** Sachen im Singular und im Plural verwendet. Es drückt Besitz oder Zugehörigkeit aus und hat immer ein Substantiv nach sich stehen.

Relativsätze mit Relativpronomen

4 Bilde aus zwei Hauptsätzen einen Hauptsatz und einen Relativsatz.

1. Look at the old woman. The woman is talking to her dog.
   Look at the old woman who is talking to her dog.
2. I've got two uncles. The two uncles are both from Saarbrücken.
3. Mum bought new flowers. The flowers were not expensive.
4. I can see a man. The man's car is green.

5 Entscheide zwischen who und which.

1. This is for German tourists ______ can't speak English.
2. The teacher ______ asked you about volleyball , is my PE teacher.
3. Luca drew a picture ______ everybody liked.
4. Thank God. We caught the train ______ was late.
5. Dad knows a lot of people ______ work as a mechanic.
6. In our forest there are a lot of trees ______ do not look very healthy.

6 Übersetze ins Deutsche.

1. I have to talk to Victor who has just bought a new computer.
2. This club is for children whose parents have to work until the evening.
3. This is our computer room which they renovated last summer.

Relativsätze ohne Relativpronomen

26

There are a lot of things	(which/that)	you can do in an amusement park.
Did you see the person	(who/whom/that)	I was talking to?
I'll tell you about the film	(which/that)	we saw in the cinema yesterday.
Look at the fotos	(which/that)	I took when I was in Berlin.

1 Lies dir die oben stehenden Beispielsätze durch und beantworte folgende Fragen. Kreuze das Zutreffende an.

1. Was sind die unterstrichenen Satzteile? ○ Subjekt ○ direktes Objekt

2. Die Informationen , die im Relativsatz gegeben werden, sind für das Verständnis des Hauptsatzes ○ nicht notwendig. ○ notwendig.

Es gibt Relativsätze, die Informationen enthalten, ohne die der Hauptsatz nicht verstanden werden kann. Diese Relativsätze nennt man **notwendige** Relativsätze. Wenn in solchen notwendigen Relativsätzen das Relativpronomen die Funktion eines direkten Objekts hat, kann das Relativpronomen auch weggelassen werden. Diese Sätze nennt man contact clauses. Sie werden vor allem in der Umgangssprache häufig benutzt.

2 Präpositionen in notwendigen Relativsätzen.
Unterstreiche das Verb **und** die Präpositionen.

1. The book () we talked about in our last German lesson is very famous.
2. The man () people in the village were afraid of died last weekend.
3. The boy () I talked to on my way home is new in our class.
4. The film () I'm interested in will be in the cinemas in November.
5. The exchange pupils () we went to Berlin with were really nice.

3 Welches Relativpronomen **könnte** in den Sätzen aus Übung 4 an der Stelle von () stehen, ist aber nicht nötig und deswegen weggefallen?

(1) *which / that* , (2) ____ , (3) ____ ,

(4) ____ , (5) ____

In notwenigen Relativsätzen können auch Präpositionen vorkommen. In contact clauses stehen die Präpositionen immer hinter dem Verb (Sätze 1-4), bzw. am Ende des Nebensatzes (Satz 5). In förmlichen Sätzen kann die Präposition auch vor dem Relativpronomen stehen: in which, to whom.

Relativsätze ohne Relativpronomen

4 Übersetze diese Sätze aus Übung 2:

1. The book () we talked about in our last German lesson is very famous.

2. The man () people in the village were afraid of died last weekend.

3. The boy () I talked to on my way home is new in our class.

5 Entscheide, ob hier ein Relativpronomen stehen muss oder nicht. Wenn keins stehen muss, lass die Lücke leer. Wenn eins fehlt, schreibe who oder which in die Lücken.

1. Dad has a friend ______ played in the UEFA Champions League.
2. I need an English teacher ______ I understand.
3. We want to buy a tent ______ is strong enough against wind and rain.
4. Most pupils ______ have a mobile send text messages very often.
5. My best friend and I only listen to music ______ we like.
6. Didn't you hear the noise ______ I was making outside?

6 Übersetze ohne Relativpronomen.

1. Ich brauche ein Handy, mit dem ich fotografieren kann.

2. Es gibt nicht viele Freunde, die ich Tag und Nacht anrufen kann.

1 Setze ein passendes Relativpronomen ein.

1. My mother is the only person ______________ I can tell the truth.
2. Have you got a computer ______________ works?
3. This is the teacher ______________ always gives so much homework.
4. Mum is a woman ______________ doesn't like shopping.

2 Verbinde die folgenden Sätze, indem du ein passendes Relativpronomen benutzt.

1. My sister wants to learn an instrument. You can play the instrument in a band.

____

____

2. Nina watched a film at the cinema. It was a love story.

____

3. Mum bought a pink T-shirt. I don't like it.

____

4. This is our neighbour. He always gets cucumbers from our garden.

____

____

3 Bilde selbst Relativsätze.

1. old people | we | visit | yesterday | be | very happy ______________________

____

2. family | live | next door | buy | a dog | last weekend ______________________

____

3. sometimes | not easy | cook | a meal | everyone | likes

____

Test 9

4

Bei welchen Relativsätzen könnte man das Relativpronomen auch weglassen? Kreuze an.

1. Most of the girls who like dancing like hip hop, too. ○
2. Where are all the tables which we carried into the classroom? ○
3. This is the boy whom I'd like to talk to. ○
4. We need an English teacher whose language is not too difficult. ○
5. The mobile which I got for my birthday is really great. ○
6. I can show you the takeaway which has the best food. ○

5

Übersetze Sätze 2., 5. und 6. aus Übung 4.

1. (Satz 2): ______________________________

____

2. (Satz 5): ______________________________

____

3. (Satz 6): ______________________________

____

6

Schreibe die folgenden contact clauses so um, dass der Relativsatz mit der Präposition beginnt (förmliche Sprache).

TIPP: Denke zuerst an das Relativpronomen, das eingesetzt werden könnte. Das brauchst du zusammen mit der Präposition für die Umformulierung.

1. Did you see the big airbus I travelled with?

Did you see the big airbus with which I travelled?

2. They sold the house we have lived in for 10 years.

____

3. That is the policeman Nick talked to after the accident yesterday.

____

Bestandsaufnahme

1 1. b), 2. c) (mehr dazu in Kapitel 1)

2 a) (mehr dazu in Kapitel 2)

3 b) (mehr dazu in Kapitel 3)

4 c) (mehr dazu in Kapitel 4)

5 b) (mehr dazu in Kapitel 5)

6 c) (mehr dazu in Kapitel 5)

7 1.b), 2. b), 3. a) (mehr dazu in Kapitel 5)

8 a) (mehr dazu in Kapitel 6)

9 1. c), 2. b), 3. a) (mehr dazu in Kapitel 7)

10 a) (mehr dazu in Kapitel 8)

11 1. b), 2.a), 3.a), 4.b) (mehr dazu in Kapitel 9)

12 1.c), 2.b) (mehr dazu in Kapitel 10)

13 b) (mehr dazu in Kapitel 11)

14 a) (mehr dazu in Kapitel 12)

15 1. b), 2. a) (mehr dazu in Kapitel 13)

16 b) (mehr dazu in Kapitel 14)

17 (mehr dazu in Kapitel 17)
3. break, 5. go, 6. say, 8. tell, 9. have

18 b) (mehr dazu in Kapitel 19)

19 b) (mehr dazu in Kapitel 20)

20 c) (mehr dazu in Kapitel 21)

21 b) (mehr dazu in Kapitel 22)

22 a) (mehr dazu in Kapitel 24)

23 1. b), 2. a), 3. c)
(mehr dazu in Kapitel 25)

1 *Question tags*

1 1c, 2d, 3b, 4a, 5f, 6e ✓

2 1b, 2a, 3d, 4c ✓

3 1. isn't she?, 2. hasn't she? 3. didn't we?, 4. did she?, 5. wasn't he?, 6. doesn't he?, 7. aren't they?, 8. have they?

4 1. isn't it?, aren't they?
2. didn't they?, did they?
3. aren't you?, didn't you?

2 *One / ones*

1. 1. one, one; 2. one, one; 3. one; 4. ones

Wenn man in einem Gespräch ein zählbares Substantiv nicht wiederholen möchte, kann man es im Englischen durch das Stützwort **one** (Singular) oder **ones** (Plural) ersetzen.

2. 1d, 2a, 3e, 4c, 5b

3. 1. which one, 2. which one, 3. which one, 4. which ones

4. 1. cheap ones, blue ones; 2. grey one, white one; 3. tall / big one, one with the hat

3 Adjektive Steigerung auf *-er* und *-est*

1. 1. Dad is quite old, but Mum is older than Dad, and Grandpa is the oldest person in our family.
   2. Mrs Brown is a nice teacher. Mrs White is nicer. Mr Black is the nicest teacher.
   3. It's hot in Italy. It's hotter in Spain. The hottest countries are in Africa.
   4. English is easy. German is easier. Maths is the easiest subject at school.

Bei der **Steigerung** der meisten einsilbigen Adjektive und manchen zweisilbigen Adjektiven wird an das Adjektiv -er oder -est angehängt.

3. 1. bigger, 2. younger, 3. not as cheap as, 4. easier, 5. The best, 6. poorer, 7. as big as, 8. older

4. a) 1. nice – nicer – (the) nicest, 2. clean – cleaner – (the) cleanest, 3. dirty – dirtier – (the) dirtiest, 4. hot – hotter – (the) hottest, 5. high – higher – (the) highest, 6. easy – easier – (the) easiest

   b) 1. nett, schön; 2. der / die / das sauberste, am saubersten 3. schmutziger / dreckiger, 4. heißer, 5. hoch, 6. der / die / das leichteste, am leichtesten

5. 1. cleverer, 2. better, 3. happiest, 4. coldest, 5. proud, 6. easier, 7. later, 8. youngest

4 Adjektive: Steigerung mit *more* und *most*

1. **einsilbig:** quick – schnell; good – gut; late – spät; great – großartig; nice - nett
   zweisilbig: stupid – dumm; famous – berühmt; careful – vorsichtig; brilliant – hervorragend; boring – langweilig
   dreisilbig: interesting – interessant; beautiful – hübsch; difficult – schwierig; dangerous – gefährlich; expensive – teuer

2. 1. Dad is careful. Mum is more careful. My brother is the most careful driver in our f amily.
   2. France is beautiful. Spain is more beautiful. Ireland is the most beautiful country in the world.

Bei der **Steigerung** aller drei- und mehrsilbigen Adjektive und den meisten zweisilbigen Adjektiven wird dem Adjektiv **more** oder **the most** vorangestellt.

4 1. more popular, the most popular; 2. more famous, the most famous; 3. better, the best; 4. sunnier, the sunniest; 5. longer, the longest; 6. more careful, the most careful; 7. worse, the worst; 8. more interesting, the most interesting

5 1. bigger than, 2. as intelligent as, 3. more famous than, 4. cleverer than, 5. not as good as

6 1. Das Wetter in Großbritannien ist nicht so schön wie in Spanien.
2. Mein bester Freund ist 12 und ich bin auch 12. Also ist er so alt wie ich.

Test 1

1 (Kapitel 1)
1. are they?, 2. aren't you?, 3. hasn't she?, 4. don't you?, 5. didn't he?, 6. wasn't she?

2 (Kapitel 2)
1. Die mit den roten Haaren; 2. Das neue ist meins. 3. aber die da drüben; 4. eine braune und zwei schwarze

3 (Kapitel 3)
1. nicer, 2. funniest; 3. worst, 4. better, 5. younger, taller

4 (Kapitel 3)
bad – worse – the worst
hot – hotter – the hottest
happy – happier – the happiest
careful – more careful – the most careful

5 (Kapitel 4)
1. They are the best boy group in the world.
2. They are the most beautiful dancers.
3. They have got the craziest shoes.
4. They are the most famous boys in Germany.

6 (Kapitel 4)
1. nicht so hoch wie – not as high as; 2. nicht so schnell wie – not as quick as; 3. so teuer wie – as expensive as; 4. schwieriger als – more difficult than 5. viel größer als – much bigger than; 6. heißer als – hotter than; 7. der schlechteste – the worst

Lösungen

5 Adverbien auf *-ly* und unregelmäßige Adverbien

1 1. beautifully, 2. quickly, 3. badly, 4. slowly, 5. carefully, 6. nicely

Ein Adjektiv beschreibt eine **Person** oder einen **Gegenstand**, also ein Nomen, näher. Ein **Adverb** beschreibt eine **Tätigkeit**, bzw. ein Verb näher. Aus vielen Adjektiven kann man ein Adverb bilden, indem man **-ly** anhängt.
Bei Adjektiven, die auf **-y** enden, lautet die Adverbendung -ily.

2 1a) schneller, 1b) schnell; 2a) harte, 2b) hart; 3a) hoher, 3b) hoch

3 1. slowly, 2. wonderfully, 3. badly, 4. right, 5. quietly, 6. well, 7. fast, 8. clearly, 9. nicely, 10. angrily

4 1. lucky, good, slowly, clearly; 2. well, quickly; 3. slowly, fast; 4. beautifully, beautiful; 5. carefully; 6. slow, easily

5
1. You can swim well.
2. Tim is a good friend.
3. Valerie laughed happily.
4. Can you speak more slowly, please?
5. Mum always drives carefully.

6 Steigerung und Vergleiche mit Adverbien

1 Peter eats <u>fast</u>. Becca eats <u>faster</u>, but Ben eats <u>the fastest</u>. Lucy eats <u>slowly</u>. Mike eats <u>more slowly</u>, but Grandma eats the <u>most slowly</u>.

Die Steigerung der Adverbien folgt den gleichen Regeln wie die Steigerung der Adjektive: Adverbien mit mehr als einer Silbe, das sind alle Adverbien mit der **Endung** -ly, werden mit **more** und **the most** gesteigert. Nur einsilbige **Adverbien** werden wie einsilbige Adjektive mit **-er** und **-est** gesteigert.

2 **Adjektiv:** good – better – the best, bad – worse – the worst
Adverb: well – better – the best, badly – more badly, the most badly

3 1. as beautifully as, 2. more clearly than, 3. the most beautifully

4 (1) nice, (2) good, (3) well, (4) cleverer, (5) easy, (6) quietly, (7) carefully, (8) tidier, (9) more quickly, (10) correct, (11) beautiful, (12) loudly, (13) well, (14) good

5 1. Adverb: more slowly; 2. Adverb: more clearly; 3. Adverb: faster / more quickly; 4. Adjektiv: bad, Adverb: well; 5. Adverb: as well as;

7 Präpositionen

1

1. The green monster is under the bed.
2. The yellow monster is behind the wardrobe.
3. The pink monster is on the wardrobe.
4. The blue monster is in the bag.
5. The red monster is in front of the computer.

2

1. at school, 2. into the house, 3. zu Hause, 4. by train, 5. at work, 6. to Stuttgart,

3

1. 2. 3. 4. 5. 6.

4

(1) to, (2) in front of, (3) before, (4) at, (5) before, (6) After, (7) to, (8) next to, (9) between

5

1. Where are you going? To Frankfurt.
2. I get up at six o'clock in the morning.
3. We go to school by bus.
4. My sister is at school, too.
5. I m never at home before 12 o'clock.
6. My father is at work.

Test 2

1

(Kapitel 5)
Yesterday my good friend Mona visited me. She lives next to the little shop in Rock Street. She wanted to see my new rabbit. We opened the cage quietly and gave it some fresh, green lettuce.Then Mona wanted to hold it because it was so soft. I showed her how: You walk slowly towards it. Then you grab it firmly by its neck and lift it up carefully. Mona picked it up, but then it jumped down and hopped over the old fence into our neighbour's garden. We had to look for it quickly because it was late. But we found it and put it back into its safe cage. Mona and I were happy because we found the rabbit again.

Adjektiv		Adverb
good	little	quietly
new	fresh	slowly
green	soft	firmly
old	late	carefully
safe	happy	quickly

2 (Kapitel 5)
a) right, b) fast, c) long, d) hard, e) early

3 (Kapitel 6)
1. Mike can run quickly.
2. Mike can't sing well / beautifully.
3. Mike can work hard.
4. Mike can't play the guitar quietly.
5. Mike can speak English well.
6. Mike can laugh happily.

4 (Kapitel 5 / 6)
slowly – more slowly – the most slowly
beautifully – more beautifully – the most beautifully
fast – faster – the fastest
carefully – more carefully – the most carefully

5 (Kapitel 3 / 5)
1. good – better – the best; bad – worse – the worst
2. well und badly
3. well – better – the best; badly – more badly – the most badly

6 (Kapitel 7)
1c), 2b), 3a), 4a), 5 c)

8 Zahlen

1 a / one hundred – einhundert
a / one thousand – eintausend / tausend
ten thousand – zehntausend
a / one hundred thousand – einhunderttausend, hunderttausend
a / one million – eine Million
a / one billion – eine Milliarde

1. Englische Zahlen werden in einzelnen Wörtern geschrieben.
2. Zwischen Hundertern und Zehnern kann ein **and** stehen.
3. Vor hundred und thousand muss ein **a / an** stehen.
4. Bei Zahlen ab Tausend wird als Tausendertrennzeichen ein **Komma** gesetzt. In deutschen Zahlen steht als Tausendertrennzeichen ein **Punkt**.
5. Aufgepasst! One billion ist im Deutschen **eine Milliarde**!

2 1c), 2d) 3b), 4e), 5g), 6a), 7f)

3 1. 40,000; 2. 75,000; 3. 86,400; 4. 10,000; 5. 1,609; 6. 8,000,000,000; 7. 384,000; 8. 365

4 a) one hundred and eleven
b) four hundred and forty-four
c) seven thousand two hundred and seventy-nine
d) twelve thousand three hundred and eighty-eight
e) two hundred and twelve thousand seven hundred and sixty-seven
f) one million eight hundred and ninety-seven thousand four hundred and thirteen
g) three billion eight hundred million five hundred thousand two hundred

9 *Some* und *any* in Aussagen und Fragen

1 1e), 2c), 3b), 4a), 5d)

2 **Bejahte Sätze:** I want to invite some friends. He is getting some drinks for us.
Fragen: Have you got any ideas? Have you got any money?
Verneinte Sätze: Sorry, I haven't got any money.

3 I want to invite <u>some</u> friends. He is getting <u>some</u> drinks for us.
Have you got <u>any</u> ideas? Have you got <u>any</u> money?
Sorry, I haven't got <u>any</u> money.

Im Englischen benutzt man **some** oder **any** um eine **unbestimmte** Menge oder Anzahl von etwas auszudrücken, im Deutschen sagt man etwas, einige oder **ein paar.** In **bejahten** Sätzen setzt man dafür some ein, in **verneinten** Sätzen und in Fragen meistens any. In manchen Fällen werden some und any im Deutschen auch gar nicht übersetzt.

4 1. some, 2. any, some, 3. any, 4. any, any, 5. any, some, 6. some (höfliches Angebot), 7. some (höfliche Bitte)

5 1. Nick hasn't got any brilliant ideas.
2. Nora hasn't got any stupid friends.
3. Oh no, you didn't buy any milk!
4. I didn't have any problems with the computer.

6 1. Hast du Neuigkeiten?
2. Ich brauche keine Hobbys.
3. Wir brauchen Eier für den Kuchen.

Lösungen

10 Zusammensetzungen mit *some* und *any, every* und *no*

1 anyone, anybody, anything, anywhere
everyone, everybody, everything. everywhere
no one (Vorsicht: no one wird nicht zusammen geschrieben!), nobody, nothing, nowhere

2 1. (irgend)jemand, 2. (irgend)etwas, 3. irgendwo

Für die Verwendung der **Zusammensetzungen** von some und any gelten die gleichen Regeln wie für **some** und **any.** Alle Zusammensetzungen mit some werden in **bejahten** Sätzen verwendet, während alle Zusammensetzungen mit any in **verneinten** Sätzen und **Fragen** verwendet werden.

3 1. everything, 2. Everybody, 3. everywhere

4 1. niemand, 2. nichts, 3. nirgends

5 1. Let's ask somebody.
2. Anything else?
3. What's the matter? – Nothing.
4. I didn't know anybody.

6 1. anything, 2. anybody, 3. somebody / someone, 4. everything, 5. something, 6. everybody

7 (1) anywhere, (2) somewhere, (3) anybody, (4) nowhere, (5) nobody, (6) Everybody, (7) somebody

11 Mengenangaben und nicht zählbare Substantive

1

bestimmte Mengenangaben (9)	unbestimmte Mengenangaben (6)
two bottles of – zwei Flaschen	not much – nicht viel
a glass of – ein Glas	some – etwas
one bar of – ein Riegel	much – viel
a pound of – ein Pfund	a lot of – viel / viele
one glass of – ein Glas	no – kein / keine
two cups of – zwei Tassen	little – wenig
two tins of – zwei Dosen	
one packet of – ein Päckchen/eine Tüte	
a piece of – ein Stück	

3 1. two glasses of orange lemonade, 2. some sugar, 3. a packet of chocolate biscuits, 4. no new information, 5. four pounds of fresh butter, 6. not much money

4 1. falsch, 2. richtig, 3. richtig, 4. richtig, 5. falsch
a) There weren't many mistakes in my test.
b) Can I have some / a glass of milk, please?

5 1. There are five tins of dog food in the cupboard.
2. I can eat three bars of chocolate in a /one minute.
3. I need four packets of crisps for my birthday.

Test 3

1 (Kapitel 8)
1. 1954, 1974, 1990; 2. 98,800; 3. 250,000

2 (Kapitel 8)
a) the second, b) twelve, c) thirteen, d) twenty-three, e) the twentieth, f) the thirty-first, g) forty, h) one billion, i) four hundred thousand, j) one hundred and one

3 (Kapitel 9)
1. some, any; 2. some; 3. any, some; 4. any, some; 5. any; 6. some

4 (Kapitel 10)
1. somebody / someone, anybody / anyone; 2. nothing, everything; 3. anything, nothing; 4. somewhere, anywhere; 5. Everybody / Everyone, Nobody / No-one

5 (Kapitel 10)
1. I want to invite everybody.
2. Dad doesn't want to invite anybody.
3. My sister wants to organise everything.
4. We need a party room somewhere.
5. Nobody wants to listen to oldies.

6 (Kapitel 9)
1. some sugar, 2. little sugar, 3. much sugar, 4. no sugar, 5. one packet of sugar, 6. one pound of sugar;

7 (Kapitel 9)
1. eggs, 2. cake

Lösungen

12 *will-future*

1 Vorhersage: Satz 1
Vermutung: Satz 2., Satz 3.
Spontane Äußerung: Satz 4.

Das will-future benutzt man 1. für **Vorhersagen**, besonders beim Wetter, 2. für **Vermutungen**, die mit I think, I hope oder I'm sure beginnen und 3. für **spontane Äußerungen.**

2 1. won't rain, 2. will make, 3. will start, 4. will win, 5. won't be

3 Good evening, ladies and gentlemen. Tomorrow we will have a warm and sunny day. There will be sunshine in the south all day. We'll have sunshine and a few clouds in the middle of the country, but it will stay warm and it won't rain. It'll be windy in the north and there will be some rain in the afternoon. Well, what will the temperatures be like? We'll have about 20 degrees in the south and in the middle. Only in the north there will be 15-18 degrees. The weather will stay warm and friendly for the whole week.

4
1. I'm sure she won't forget it.
2. It will rain in the afternoon.
3. I'm sure they won't write a test tomorrow.
4. Paul won't take the train to London.
5. There will be a storm tonight.

5
1. I'm sure I'll be first in the race.
2. Maria won't eat vegetables again.
3. It'll rain and it'll be very cold.
4. The restaurants won't be open on Sunday.

13 *if*-Sätze Typ I

1 1d), 2c), 3e), 4a), 5b)

2
1. Wenn es schneit, trage ich meine neuen Stiefel. / werde ich meine neuen Stiefel tragen.
2. Ich schaue mir den Film hier an, wenn es OK ist.

3 1c), 2a), 3b)

4 1. will catch, 2. are not / aren't, 3. will feel, 4. will get;

5 1. don't learn, 2. will call, 3 comes, 4. won't play

6 1. is, will drive; 2. won't get, lose; 3. find, will be; 4. will call, want.

Test 4

1 (Kapitel 12)
1. Wait a moment. I'll help you.
2. No milk? I'll buy two bottles in the supermarket.
3. My leg hurts. OK, I'll call the doctor.

2 (Kapitel 12)
(1) will be, (2)will rain, (3) won't stop, 84) will start, (5) will see, (6) won't rain
(7) will come, (8) will be, (9) will become, (10) will have

3 (Kapitel 12)
1. Ich bin sicher, dass Mama eine Geburtstagsparty für mich vorbereitet.
2. Ich glaube, ich kaufe ihr eine paar Blumen.
3. Ich hoffe, wir bekommen morgen keine Hausaufgaben (auf).

4 (Kapitel 13)
1. bake, will make; 2. invite, will have; 3. don't buy, will be; 4. doesn't come, won't have

5 (Kapitel 13)
1. If it snows tomorrow, I will build a snowman.
2. If we write an English test tomorrow, I will / won't write a bad mark.
3. If my parents give me more pocket money, I will go to the cinema more often.
4. If Mark does my homework for me, I will be very happy.

6 (Kapitel 13)
1. Ich backe dir einen Kuchen, wenn du willst.
2. Meine Schwester spielt nicht in der Band / wird nicht in der Band spielen, wenn sie sich nicht besser fühlt.
3. Die Freundin meiner Mutter schneidet dir die Haare / wird dir die Haare schneiden, wenn du sie nett fragst.

14 *Present perfect*

1 1c (never), 2a (already), 3e (for), 4d (not...yet), 5f (just), 6b (since)

2
1. Wir haben zehn Jahre lang in Berlin gelebt.
2. Wir leben seit (dem Jahr) 2000 in Berlin.

3
1. Nico has already fed the cat.
2. Nico has already phoned Grandma.
3. Nico hasn't thought of a birthday present for Luke yet.
4. Nico has bought ten eggs and a lettuce at the market.
5. Nico has already taken Mum's letters to the post office.
6. Nico hasn't put his clothes into the wardrobe yet.
7. Nico hasn't cleaned his football shoes yet.
8. Nico has already learnt / learned his vocabulary.

TIPP: Hast du daran gedacht, dass du bei den Sätzen 6. 7. und 8 ein his statt des your verwenden musst?

4
1. I have never been to Great Britain.
2. We bought a dog yesterday.
3. We have just come back from Berlin.

15 *Present perfect:* Fragen und Kurzantworten

1 1. Unterstrichen werden: have done, 've done, Have decided, 've booked

2
Jessica: ... hast ... schon gemacht?
Jane: ... habe ... schon gemacht.
Jessica: ... Hast ... entschieden...?
Jane: ...habe ... reserviert.

3
1. b und e,
2. c und f,
3. a und d

Im Deutschen werden manche Perfektformen mit **haben** (z.B. ich **habe** gegessen, er **hat** gegessen, ihr **habt** gegessen) und manche Perfektformen mit **sein** (z.B. ich **bin** geflogen, er **ist** geflogen, ihr **seid** geflogen) gebildet. Im Englischen steht für jede Perfektform immer have / has + 3.Form!

4
1. Yes, I have. / No, I haven't.
2. Yes, I have. / No, I haven't.
3. Yes, he / she has. / No, he / she hasn't.
4. Yes, they have. / No, they haven't.

5 1a. already Hast du schon ein Geschenk zum Geburtstag deiner Mutter gekauft?
1b. n't ... yet Nein, ich habe noch keine gute Idee gehabt.
2a. ever Warst du jemals / schon mal in Berlin?
2b. already Ja, ich habe schon mal eine ganze Woche dort verbracht.
3a. ever Bist du jemals / schon mal in einem Hubschrauber geflogen?
3b. never Nein, ich bin noch nie in einem Hubschrauber oder einem Flugzeug geflogen.

16 Im Vergleich: *simple past* und *present perfect*

1 Signalwörter für das simple past in den Sätzen 1. (last Friday), 4. (three years ago), 5. (in 1888), 9. (an hour ago), 10. (yesterday)
Signalwörter für das present perfect in den Sätzen 2. (for), 3. (n't ... yet), 6. (since), 7. (ever), 8. (just)

2

Signalwörter für das simple past	Signalwörter für das present perfect
1. last Friday	2. for
3. three years ago	4. not yet
5. in 1888	6. since
7. an hour ago	8. ever
9. yesterday	10. just

3
1. letzten Freitag
3. vor drei Jahren
4. 1888
5. vor einer Stunde
7. gestern

2. seit
4. noch nicht
6. seit
8. jemals
10. gerade

4
1. missed, was
2. hasn't been, broke
3. Have (you) cleaned, cleaned
4. finished, Have (you already) finished
5. booked, haven't booked

5
1. Mark hasn't finished his homework yet.
2. I didn't go to New York last summer.
3. The train didn't arrive at 8 o'clock.
4. I haven't called the doctor (yet)

6
1. Did you sleep well last night?
2. Did you like Jim's party last weekend?
3. Have you ever been to an amusement park?
4. Have you ever eaten Sauerkraut in Germany?

Lösungen

17 Unregelmäßige Verben

1 **Regelmäßige Verben:** 1. work, 2. walk, 3. arrive, 4. bark, 5. help
Unregelmäßige Verben:
6. wake, woke woken
7. ride, rode, ridden
8. read, read, read
9. make, made, made
10. sleep, slept, slept

2

1. gew nnen: w n – w n – won	2. verl ren: l se – l st – lost
3. z chnen: draw – dr w – dr wn	4. fli en: fl – fl w – fl wn
5. spr chen: sp k – spoke – sp ken	6. re en: run – r n – run
7. b deuten: m n – m nt – meant	8. verl tzen, weh tun: h rt – hurt – h rt
9. tr nk n: dr nk – dr nk – dr nk	10. n men: t ke – t k – t k n

3

1. tell, told, told	wie	sell, sold, sold
2. keep, kept, kept	wie	sleep, slept, slept
3. send, sent, sent	wie	spend, spent, spent
4. cut, cut, cut	wie	shut, shut, shut
5. teach, taught, taught	wie	catch, caught, caught
6. fight, fought, fought	wie	think, thought, thought
7. know, knew, known	wie	throw, threw, thrown
8. take, took, taken	wie	shake, shook, shaken

4 1. swim, 2. go, 3. leave, 4. meet, 5. choose, 6. do, 7. be, 8. eat

5 1. caught, caught, (fangen) 2. taught, taught, (unterrichten) 3. bought, bought, (kaufen) 4. brought, brought, (bringen) 5. fought, fought, (kämpfen) 6. thought, thought (denken)

6
1. drive, drove, driven
2. shut, shut, shut / close, closed, closed
3. have, had, had
4. understand, understood, understood
5. bring, brought, brought
6. smell, smelt, smelt

7

S	D	O	N	E	P	O	S	A	W	Z	E	W	A
F	E	E	L	J	K	M	O	F	V	W	O	R	N
P	U	R	E	T	H	R	O	W	F	E	W	A	S
E	A	S	A	Y	B	R	O	K	T	A	K	E	N
G	I	M	N	T	E	A	C	H	K	E	R	T	S
O	S	H	O	W	N	G	A	T	E	N	G	E	T
B	E	C	A	M	E	H	O	L	P	E	R	N	T
F	A	K	N	E	W	L	E	D	R	I	V	E	N

Grundform	simple past Form	past participle Form
1. feel	felt	felt
2. throw	threw	thrown
3. say	said	said
4. teach	taught	taught
5. get	got	got
see	6. saw	seen
be	7. was	been
eat	8. ate	eaten
become	9. became	become
know	10. knew	known
do	did	11. done
wear	wore	12. worn
take	took	13. taken
show	showed	14. shown
drive	drove	15. driven

Lösungen

Test 5

1 (Kapitel 14)
1. Have you already eaten lunch?
2. My brother hasn't repaired my bike yet.
3. Have you ever been to Paris?
4. I've never been to a museum.
5. I've just washed your new jeans.
6. ave you ever had a pet?

2 (Kapitel 15)
1. Yes, I have. 2. No, I haven't.
3. Yes, I have. 4. No, they haven't.
5. Yes, he / she has. 6. No, I haven't.
7. No, he / she hasn't. 8. Yes, we have.

3 (Kapitel 16)
1. Have (you) checked, checked, haven't got
2. has stayed
3. bought, has looked
4. have (just) finished, Have (you) finished
5. have (just) spoken
6. have lived

4 (Kapitel 16)
simple past: understood, didn't forget, felt, didn't make
present perfect: haven't taken, has broken, has phoned, hasn't eaten

5 (Kapitel 17)
1. wrote, written 2. read, read
3. paid, paid 4. had, had
5. felt, felt 6. found, found
7. told, told 8. did, done
9. was / were, been 10. taught, taught

18 *would, could, Would you like...?*

1 1b, 2a, 3h, 4i, 5g, 6e, 7f, 8d, 9c

2
1. Was könnten wir tun?
2. Wir könnten in den Park gehen und könnten ein Eis essen.
3. Was würdest du im Fernsehen anschauen, die Liebesgeschichte oder die Talkshow?
4. Ich würde mir nicht die Liebesgeschichte anschauen, ich würde die Talkshow anschauen.
5. Wo könnten wir übernachten?
6. Wir könnten auf einem Campingplatz übernachten. Das wäre großartig!

3

1. Würdest du dieses weiße T-Shirt kaufen?
2. Könntest du bitte das Fenster schließen?
3. Oma würde keinen Computer wollen.
4. Wir könnten Celine anrufen. Sie weiß alles.
5. Wir könnten nach einer Gruppenfahrkarte fragen. Das wäre nicht so teuer.

4

1. I would go to the concert with you.
2. We could ask Mum. She could pick us up.
3. Could you help Nicole, please?
4. Vera could make a salad and I could bake a pizza.
5. Joe wouldn't play tricks on us.

19 *Gerund* als Subjekt und *gerund* als Objekt

1

1. Playing football, Basketballspielen
2. jogging / running, Joggen, Laufen

Gerunds werden aus Verben + **ing** gebildet. Sie verwandeln sich damit zu **Nomen** (swim —> swimming). Das geht auch im Deutschen (schwimmen —> das Schwimmen). Manchmal muss man ein gerund im Deutschen umschreiben, z.B. ‚das Schreiben von Postkarten' oder ‚E-Mails zu schreiben' ...etc. Das gerund als Subjekt steht am Satzanfang. Ihm folgt meistens das **Verb *be***. Vor einem gerund steht im Englischen kein **Artikel**! Beachte auch besondere Schreibweisen:
Konsonanten am Wortende werden oft **verdoppelt**, *-e* am Verbende fällt weg.

2

1. playing computer games
2. repairing bikes
3. talking on the phone
4. listening to music

Ein gerund kann auch **Objekt** in einem Satz sein. Dabei steht es vor allem nach Verben, die eine **Vorliebe** (like, love, enjoy) oder eine **Abneigung** (don't like, hate) ausdrücken und nach einigen Sonderfällen (u.a. How about...?)

3

1. Going to the cinema is my favourite activity.
2. I'm very interested in collecting football cards.
3. I love watching TV in bed on Saturdays.

4

1. My hobbies are swimming and playing tennis.
2. Sometimes playing the piano is boring.
3. Martha and John enjoy having holidays.
4. What can we do? – How about playing cards?
5. I'm not interested in dancing. I can't stand dancing.

Test 6

1

(Kapitel 18)
Mum: Good morning, Mike. Would you sit down here, please?
Mike: Good morning. Could I have a spoon, please? I would like to eat muesli.
Mum: Here you are. Would you like to have toast after that?
Mike: Yes, maybe. Could I have some milk, please?
Mum: Would you like to have cheese on your sandwich?
Mike: Yes, Cheese is OK. Thank you.

2

(Kapitel 18)
1. Could you tell me what time it is, please?/ Could you tell me the time, (please)?
2. Could you tell me where the next bus station is, (please)?
3. Would/ Could you show me the way, (please)?

3

(Kapitel 19)
1. sitting, 2. travelling, 3. running, 4. preparing, 5. swimming, 6. smiling, 7. dancing, 8. leaving, 9. cutting, 10. driving

4

(Kapitel 19)
1. Wie wär's mit Bungeespringen?
2. Ich kann das saubermachen von Fußballschuhen nicht ausstehen./ Ich kann es nicht ausstehen Fußballschuhe sauber zu machen.
3. Mama genießt Kochen sehr./ Mama genießt es sehr zu kochen.
4. Reisen ist wirklich klasse/ großartig.

5

(Kapitel 19)
1. I hate repairing bikes.
2. I love writing long letters.
3. I don't like learning vocabulary.
4. I enjoy sleeping a lot at the weekend.
5. I'm interested in drawing.
6. I can't stand playing football.

20 *to be able to, to be allowed to, to have to*

1 can – können, may – dürfen, must – müssen

2 Alle Aussagen (1.-6.) müssen angekreuzt werden!

4

Ersatzform in verschiedenen Zeiten	Welche Zeit ist es?	Von welchem *modal* ist es die Ersatzform?
1. (I) wasn't able to	simple past	can (not)
2. (you) have to	simple present	must
3. (they) didn't have to	simple past	must (not)
4. (we) were allowed to	simple past	may
5. (she) doesn't have to	simple present	must (not)
6. (I) wasn't allowed to	simple past	may (not)
7. (they) were able to	simple past	can
8. (I) won't be allowed to	will-future	may (not)
9. (I) will be able to	will-future	can
10. (he) will be allowed to	will-future	may

5
1. I had to do a lot of homework yesterday.
2. Bob was allowed to go to the cinema last Saturday.
3. Dad is able to repair Tina's bike.

6
1. Mum will be able to drive us to the concert.
2. You will be allowed to go to the zoo.
3. My sister will have to phone her teacher.

21 *Past progressive:* Sätze mit *while* und *when*

1 While the two school teams were playing, it started to rain. Dave was running across the field when Max fell on the grass. While Max was holding his left leg, the trainer called the ambulance. When the ambulance came, a lot of players were standing around Max.

2 Das **past progressive** wird mit einer Form von **be** im simple past (**was / were**) + ing-Form gebildet. Die **Verneinung** im past progressive wird mit **wasn't / weren't** + ing-Form gebildet.

3 While und when leiten Nebensätze ein, auf die ein Hauptsatz folgt. Dabei gelten für beide Konjunktionen unterschiedliche Regeln:
Im while-Satz steht das **past progressive**, es folgt ein Haupsatz im **simple past.**
Im when-Satz steht das **simple past,** es folgt ein Hauptsatz mit **past progressive.**

4 1. were playing, 2. started, 3. was running, 4. fell, 5. was holding, 6. called, 7. came, 8. were standing, 9. carried, 10. was talking, 11. were singing, 12. clapping, 13. scored, 14. was trying, 15. stopped, 16. left, 17. were still singing

5 When Mrs Rolix entered the classroom, …
1. … two girls were eating their sandwiches.
2. … five boys were sitting on the table.
3. … one girl was standing on a chair.
4. … two girls were laughing.
5. … one boy was throwing a ball.

Test 7

1 (Kapitel 20)
1. was allowed to, 2. had to, 3. was able to, 4. had to, 5. will have to, 6. won't be allowed to

2 (Kapitel 20)
1. I can understand that / it.
2. I couldn't understand that / it.
3. I won't be able to understand that / it.
4. You must learn that by heart.
5. We had to learn that by heart.
6. You will have to learn that by heart.
7. I wasn't allowed to call / phone you.
8. You may go home.

3 (Kapitel 20)
1.b – dürfen, 2.d – können, 3.a – müssen, 4.c – dürfen

4 (Kapitel 21)
1. was playing, 2. were standing, 3. were eating, 4. was talking, 5. was laughing, 6. were selling

5 (Kapitel 21)
1. was preparing, came, 2. was doing, went out, 3. landed, was raining, 4. were writing, knocked

6 (Kapitel 21)
1. When I went out of the house, the sun was shining.
2. While I was watching TV, my mobile rang.
3. When we arrived at the station, a lot of football fans were singing there.

22 *going to-future*

1
1. **Frage:** What are you going to do this weekend?
2. **Aussage:** I'm going to relax.
3. **Verneinte Aussage:** I'm not going to do anything.

3
1. Was machst du dieses Wochenende? / Was wirst du am Wochenende tun?
2. Ich werde ausspannen. / Ich spanne aus / erhole mich.
3. Ich werde nichts tun. / Ich tue nichts.

4
1. are going to visit, 2. are going to stay, 3. is going to cook, 4. are going to set, 5. am going to go

5
1. Are you going to bake a cake for your grandparents?
2. Are you going to tell them about your last English test?

6
1. Ich werde meine neue Hose und meine neuen Schuhe tragen.
2. Ich werde Sandra bitten Ihre Kamera mitzubringen.
3. Tim wird DJ sein. Also werden wir tolle Musik hören.
4. Ich werde nicht vor 22 Uhr nach Hause gehen.

23 Im Vergleich: *will-future* und *going to-future*

1
3. We hope it won't rain tomorrow.
4. We're going to go to France next summer.
5. I'm going to tell you my marks.
6. It's so hot here. – I'll get you a drink.

will-future	going to-future
will meet	're going to be
won't rain	're going to go
'll get	'm going to tell

Das **will-future** wird für alle Personen im Singular und im Plural mit will + Grundform gebildet. Die Verneinung wird für alle Personen im Singular und Plural mit won't + Grundform gebildet. Das **going to-future** wird in bejahten und verneinten Aussagen so gebildet:
- eine Form von be + going to + Infinitiv des Verbs
- eine verneinte Form von be + going to + Infinitiv des Verbs

2
Das will-future benutzt man 1. für **Vorhersagen**, besonders beim Wetter, 2. für **Vermutungen**, die mit I think, I hope oder I'm sure beginnen und 3. für **spontane Äußerungen**. Das going to-future wird verwendet, wenn man einen **Plan** oder eine **Idee** für ein zukünftiges Ereignis hat. Es wird außerdem für Vorhersagen verwendet, wenn es deutliche Anzeichen für das tatsächliche Eintreten des Ereignisses gibt.

3 und 4

Satz	will-future			going to-future	
	spontane Entscheidung	Wetter-vorhersage	Vermutungen mit *I'm sure, I think, I hope*	Plan, Idee	Vorhersage mit deutlichen Anzeichen
1.					X
2.		X			
3.			X		
4.				X	
5.				X	
6.			X		
7.	X				
8.		X			

5
1. Mum, there's someone at the door. – Wait, I'll open the door.
2. We're going to have a great party.
3. I'm sure we'll win.

24 Possessivpronomen

1
Possessivbegleiter (blau) bei den Sätzen 1 (my), 2. (your), 4. (her), 7. (their), 8. (your), 9. (his) 14. (our), 15. (its)
Possessivpronomen (grün) in den Sätzen 3 (yours), 5. (hers), 6. (mine), 10. (theirs), 11. (ours), 12. (yours), 13. (its), 16. (his)

2
Possessivbegleiter: my, your, his, her, its, our, your, their
Possessivpronomen: mine, yours, his, hers, its, ours, yours, theirs

3
1. Is that my seat? Yes, that is yours.
2. I can't find my book. You can take / have mine.
3. Whose CDs are these? They are ours, thank you.

4
1. you, 2. our, 3. my, 4. yours, 5. mine, 6. you, 7 your, 8. We, 9. us, 10. yours, 11. mine, 12. hers, 13. His, 14. your, 15. my, 16. my, 17. your

Test 8

1 (Kapitel 23)
1. I'll wait, 2. 's going to, 3. 're going to, 4. 'll be, 5. won't come, 6. 'll get

2 (Kapitel 12 / 23)

	spontane Entscheidung	Vermutung	Wetter-vorhersage	Plan, Idee	Vorhersage mit Anzeichen
Satz 1	X				
Satz 2					X
Satz 3				X	
Satz 4		X			
Satz 5		X			
Satz 6	X				
Satz 7			X		

3 (Kapitel 12 / 23)
1. These bags are too heavy. – Wait, I'll help you.
2. It will be sunny and dry at the weekend. It won't rain.

4 (Kapitel 22)
1. Gehst du zu Fuß zu Lisa? / Wirst du zu Lisa zu Fuß gehen?
2. Kauft dein Bruder den Computer? / Wird dein Bruder den Computer kaufen?
3. Machst du zusammen mit deinem Freund / deiner Freundin das Projekt? Wirst du zusammen mit deinem Freund / deiner Freundin das Projekt machen?

5 (Kapitel 24)
1. his, 2. theirs, 3. mine, 4. hers, 5. ours, 6. yours / his / hers / theirs / mine, 7. mine / yours / his / hers / ours / theirs

6 (Kapitel 24)
1. That's mine.
2. Those are not yours.
3. Those are **hers** now. Those are **theirs** now.
4. Are those yours?
5. Yes, they're ours.

25 Relativsätze mit Relativpronomen

1 Die **Relativpronomen** who, which und that lauten im **Singular** und **Plural** immer gleich, sie verändern sich nicht. **Who** bezieht sich aber nur auf Personen, **which** nur auf Sachen. **That** kann sowohl für Personen als auch für Sachen stehen.

4
2. I've got two uncles who are both from Saarbrücken.
3. Mum bought new flowers which were not expensive.
4. I can see a man whose car is green.

5 1. who, 2. who, 3. which, 4. which, 5. who, 6. which

6
1. Ich muss mit Victor, der sich gerade einen neuen Computer gekauft hat, sprechen.
2. Dieser Verein / Club ist für Kinder, deren Eltern bis abends arbeiten müssen.
3. Dies hier ist unser Computerraum, den sie letzten Sommer renoviert haben.

26 Relativsätze ohne Relativpronomen

1
1. Die unterstrichenen Satzteile sind **direktes Objekt**.
2. Die Informationen, die im Relativsatz gegeben werden, sind für das Verständnis des Hauptsatzes **notwendig**.

2 Zu unterstreichen sind:
1. talked about
2. were afraid of
3. talked to
4. 'm interested in
5. went ... with

3 1. which / that, 2. who / that, 3. who / that, 4. which / that, 5. who / that

4
1. Das Buch, über das wir in unserer letzten Deutschstunde gesprochen haben, ist sehr berühmt.
2. Der Mann, vor dem die Leute aus dem Dorf Angst hatten, starb letztes Wochenende.
3. Der Junge, mit dem ich auf meinem Weg nach Hause gesprochen habe, ist neu in unserer Klasse.

5
1. who
2. who
3. which
4. who
5. kein Relativpronomen nötig
6. kein Relativpronomen nötig

6
1. I need a mobile I can take photos with.
2. There are not many friends I can call day and night.

Test 9

1 (Kapitel 25)
1. who / that
2. which / that
3. who / that
4. who / that

2 (Kapitel 25)
1. My sister wants to learn an instrument which you can play in a band.
2. Nina watched a film at the cinema which was a love story.
3. Mum bought a pink T-shirt which I didn't like.
4. This is our neighbour who always gets cucumbers from our garden.

3 (Kapitel 25 / 26)
1. The old people (who) we visited yesterday were very happy.
2. The family who lives next door bought a dog last weekend.
3. It's sometimes not easy to cook a meal which everyone likes.

4 (Kapitel 25 / 26)
Bei den Sätzen 2., 3., 5. kann man das Relativpronomen auch weglassen.

5 (Kapitel 25 / 26)
1. Wo sind die ganzen Tische, die wir in den Klassenraum getragen haben?
2. Das Handy, das ich zum Geburtstag bekommen habe, ist echt klasse.
3. Ich kann dir den Imbiss zeigen, der das beste Essen hat.

6 (Kapitel 26)
1. Did you see the big airbus with which I travelled?
2. They sold the house in which we have lived for ten years.
3. That is the policeman to whom Nick talked after the accident yesterday.

Wortliste

A

a/am – ein, eine
a bag of – eine Tüte
a few – ein paar, einige, wenig
a lot – sehr, viel
a.m. – vormittags
6 a.m. – 6 Uhr morgens
about – über
accident – Unfall
across – quer über
adult – Erwachsener
after – nach
afternoon – Nachmittag
again – noch einmal
against – gegen
airport – Flughafen
alarm clock – Wecker
all (the) – alle
all day – den ganzen Tag
almost – fast
alone – allein
already – schon
always – immer
ambulance – Krankenwagen
amusement centre / park – Freizeitpark
and – und
animal – Tier
another – noch ein, eine, eins
answer – Antwort
anybody – (irgend)jemand
anyone – (irgend)jemand
anything – (irgend)etwas
anywhere – irgendwo
apple – Apfel
are – bist; seid; sind
around – um...herum
to arrive – ankommen
to ask – fragen
at – bei; an; in
at the moment – im Augenblick

B

back – zurück
bag – Schultasche
a bag of – eine Tüte ...
ball – Ball
balloon – Ballon
banana – Banane
band – Band, Musikgruppe
bank – Bank (Sparkasse)
bar – Riegel
to bark – bellen
bathroom – Badezimmer
to be – sein
to be able to – können
to be allowed to – dürfen
to be interested in – sich interessieren für
beach – Strand
to become – werden
bed – Bett
bedroom – Schlafzimmer
before – bevor
to begin – beginnen
behind – hinter
to believe – glauben
bell – Glocke
best – beste/-r/-s
to bet – wetten
better – besser
big – groß
bike – Fahrrad
billion – Milliarde
birthday – Geburtstag
black – schwarz
to blow – blasen, wehen
to blow up – in die Luft jagen
blue – blau
board – Tafel, Brett
boat – Boot
book – Buch
to book – buchen
boring – langweilig
born – geboren
to borrow – ausleihen
both – beide
bottle – Flasche
bowl – Schüssel
box – Schachtel, Karton, Kiste
boy – Junge
bread – Brot
break – Pause
to break – brechen
breakfast – Frühstück
bridge – Brücke
brilliant – hervorragend
to bring – mitbringen, bringen
British – britisch
brochure – Broschüre
brother – Bruder
brown – braun
to brush – bürsten
budgie – Wellensittich
to build – bauen, aufbauen
burger – Burger
to burn – brennen
bus (pl. buses) – Bus
bus stop – Bushaltestelle
busy – beschäftigt

but – aber
to buy – kaufen
by – mit
Bye! – Tschüs!

C

cafe – Cafe
cafeteria – Cafeteria
cage – Käfig
cake – Kuchen
call – Anruf
to call – anrufen, rufen, nennen
camera – Kamera
campsite – Campingplatz
can – können
can't stand – kann nicht ausstehen
candle – Kerze
cap – Kappe, Schirmmütze
captain – Kapitän
car – Auto
card – Karte, Spielkarte
careful – vorsichtig
caretaker – Hausmeister/-in
carrot – Karotte
to carry – tragen
cat – Katze
cat food – Katzenfutter
to catch – fangen
CD – CD
centre – Mitte, Zentrum
chair – Stuhl
championship – Wettkampf
to chase – verfolgen, jagen
cheap – billig
to cheat – mogeln
to check in – einchecken
to check out – auschecken
cheese – Käse
chicken – Huhn
child (pl. children) – Kind
chocolate – Schokolade
to choose – auswählen
Christmas – Weihnachten
church – Kirche
cinema – Kino
to clap – klatschen
class – Klasse
classroom – Klassenraum
clean – sauber
to clean – aufräumen, putzen
clever – schlau, klug
clock – Uhr
to close – schließen
closed – geschlossen
clothes – Kleidung
cloud – Wolke
club – Club, Verein
coach – Reisebus, Kutsche
coat – Mantel
coffee – Kaffee
coin – Münze
cold – kalt
to collect – sammeln
Cologne – Köln
colour – Farbe
to come – kommen
come down – herunterkommen
comic – Comic
communication – Verständigung, Kommunikation
to compare – vergleichen
competition – Wettbewerb
computer – Computer
to connect – verbinden
cook – Koch/Köchin
to cook – kochen
cool – cool, klasse
to copy – kopieren, abschreiben
corner – Ecke
cornflakes – Cornflakes
correct – richtig
to correct – korrigieren
to cost – kosten
cosy – gemütlich
could – konnte/könnte
to count – zählen
country (pl. countries) – Land
cousin – Cousin/Cousine
to cover – bedecken
cow – Kuh
cricket – Kricket
crisp – Kartoffelchip
to cross – überqueren, kreuzen
cucumber – Gurke
cupboard – Schrank
curtain – Vorhang
customer – Kunde/Kundin
to cut – schneiden
cute – süß, niedlich

D

dad – Vati, Papa
dance – Tanz
to dance – tanzen
dangerous – gefährlich
dark – dunkel
date – Datum
daughter – Tochter
day – Tag

Wortliste

dead – tot
dear – Schatz
Dear... – Liebe(r)...
December – Dezember
to decide – entscheiden
degree – Grad
department store – Kaufhaus, Warenhaus
desk – Lehrerpult, Schreibtisch
dessert – Nachtisch
dialogue – Dialog, Gespräch
diary – Tagebuch
dictionary – Wörterbuch
to die – sterben
different – anders, andere
dining-room – Esszimmer
dinner – Abendessen
dirty – dreckig
disco – (Schul-)Disko
to dive – tauchen
divorced – geschieden
to do – tun, machen
dog – Hund
dog food – Hundefutter
door – Tür
down – entlang, herunter, hinunter, nach unten
downstairs – unten (in einem Gebäude)
drama – Schauspiel
to draw – zeichnen
dream – Traum
to dream – träumen
dress – Kleid
drink – Getränk
to drink – trinken
to drive – fahren
driver – Fahrer/-in
drum – Trommel
dry – trocken
to dry – trocknen
during – während

E

each other – einander
ear – Ohr
early – früh
earth – Erde
east – Osten
Easter – Ostern
easy – einfach, leicht
to eat – essen
egg – Ei
end – Ende
to end – zu Ende gehen, enden, beenden
English – englisch, Englisch
to enjoy – genießen
enough – genug
European – Europäer/-in
even – sogar
evening – Abend
event – Veranstaltung
ever – jemals
every – jede/-r/-s
everybody – alle, jede/-r/-s
everyone – alle, jede/-r
everything – alles
everywhere – überall
example – Beispiel
exchange – Austausch
excited – aufgeregt
exciting – aufregend
Excuse me. – Entschuldigung!, Entschuldige!, Entschuldigen Sie!
exercise – Übung
exercise book – Heft
expensive – teuer
to explain – erklären
extra – extra, besonders
eye – Auge

F

face – Gesicht
fair – Fest, Markt; Jahrmarkt
fairy – Fee
to fall – fallen
false – falsch
family – Familie
famous – berühmt
far – weit
farm – Bauernhof
farmer – Bauer/Bäuerin
fast – schnell
father – Vater
favourite – Lieblings-...
February – Februar
to feed – füttern
to feel – fühlen
fence – Zaun
ferry (pl. ferries) – Fähre
festival – Festival, Fest
field – Wiese, Sportfeld
fight – Streit, Kampf
to fight – kämpfen
to fill in – ausfüllen
film – Film
finally – schließlich
to find – finden
fine – gut
finger – Finger
to finish – beenden, fertig machen

fire – Feuer
firm – fest
first – zuerst, als Erste/-r/-s, erste/-r/-s
fish (pl. fish) – Fisch
flag – Flagge
flat – Wohnung
floor – Fußboden
flour – Mehl
flower – Blume
to fly – fliegen
folder – Hefter, Mappe, Ordner
to follow – folgen
food – Lebensmittel
foot (pl. feet) – Fuß
football – Fußball
for – für
for – seit
forest – Wald
to forget – vergessen
fork – Gabel
form – Form
fox – Fuchs
free – kostenlos, frei
French – Französisch
fresh – frisch
Friday – Freitag
fridge – Kühlschrank
friend – Freund/-in
frog – Frosch
from – von, aus
fruit – Obst
full – voll
fun – Spaß
funny – lustig, komisch
furniture – Möbel

G

game – Spiel
garden – Garten
German – deutsch, Deutsch, Deutsche/-r
to get – bekommen
to get lost – sich verirren
to get to – zu/nach … kommen
to get up – aufstehen
ghost – Geist
girl – Mädchen
to give – geben
glass – Glas
to go – gehen
to go swimming – schwimmen gehen
goal – Tor
goat – Ziege
gold – Gold
good – gut
goodbye – tschüs, auf Wiedersehen
goose (pl. geese) – Gans
to grab – anfassen, packen
gram – Gramm
grammar – Grammatik
grandad – Opa
grandfather – Großvater
grandma – Oma
grandmother – Großmutter
grandpa – Opa
grandparents – Großeltern
grass – Gras
great – großartig, toll, klasse
green – grün
grey – grau
grid – Tabelle, Gitter
group – Gruppe, Klasse
to grow – wachsen
to guess – erraten, raten
guide – Führer/-in
guitar – Gitarre
guys – Leute, Jungs

H

half (pl. halves) – Hälfte
half past three – halb vier
hall – Aula, Saal, Flur
ham – Schinken
hand – Hand
to hang – hängen
to happen – passieren, geschehen
happy – fröhlich, glücklich
hard – hart, fest
hat – Hut
to have – haben
to have got – haben, besitzen
he – er
head – Kopf
headmaster – Schulleiter/-in
healthy – gesund
to hear – hören
heavy – schwer
helicopter – Hubschrauber
hello – hallo
help – Hilfe
to help – helfen
her – ihr/-e, sie, ihr
here – hier
to hide – verstecken
him – ihn, ihm
hip – Hüfte

Wortliste

his – sein/-e
to hit – treffen, schlagen
hobby – Hobby
to hold – halten
home – zu Hause
homework – Hausaufgaben
to hope – hoffen
to hop – hüpfen
horse – Pferd
hospital – Krankenhaus
hostel – Herberge
youth hostel – Jugendherberge
hot – heiß
hour – Stunde
how – wie
hungry – hungrig
hurry – Eile
to hurry – sich beeilen
Hurry up! – Beeil dich!
to hurt – verletzen, weh tun

I

I – ich
ice cream – Eis
idea – Idee, Einfall, Ahnung
idiot – Idiot/-in
ill – krank
in – in, herein, hinein
to include – beinhalten
information – Information
to be interested in – sich interessieren für
interesting – interessant
Internet – Internet
into – in, hinein
invitation – Einladung
to invite – einladen
irregular – unregelmäßig
is – ist
isn't – ist nicht
island – Insel
it – er, sie, es, ihm, ihn, ihr
Italian – italienisch, Italienisch, Italiener/-in
its – sein/-e, ihr/-e

J

jam – Marmelade
January – Januar
jeans – Jeans
joke – Witz
juice – Saft
July – Juli
jumbled – durcheinander geworfen
to jump – springen
June – Juni
just – gerade; nur

K

to keep – halten
key – Schlüssel
kid – Kind
to kill – töten
kind – Art
kiss – Kuss
to kiss – küssen
kitchen – Küche
knife (pl. knives) – Messer
to know – wissen, kennen

L

lamb – Lamm
land – Festland
language – Sprache
lantern – Laterne
large – groß
last – letzte/-r/-s
late – zu spät
later – später
to laugh – lachen
lazy – faul
to learn – lernen
to learn by heart – auswendig lernen
to leave – abfahren, verlassen
left – links, linke/-r/-s; übrig
leg – Bein
lemonade – Limonade
lesson – Unterrichtsstunde
to let – lassen
let's – lass uns/lasst uns
letter – Brief
lettuce – Salatkopf
library – Bibliothek, Bücherei
to lie – liegen, lügen
life (pl. lives) – Leben
to lift – heben
to lift sth. up – etwas hochheben
like – ähnlich, wie
to like – mögen, gern haben
line – Linie
lip – Lippe
list – Liste
to listen – zuhören, (an)hören
little – klein; wenig
to live – leben
living room – Wohnzimmer
long – lang

to look – schauen, sehen, aussehen
to look at – ansehen
to loose - verlieren
lots (of) – viel
loud – laut
to love – lieben
Love,… – Herzliche Grüße
luggage – (Reise)Gepäck
lunch – Mittagessen
lunchtime – Mittagszeit

M

magazine – Zeitschrift
to make – machen, tun
man (pl. men) – Mann
manager – Geschäftsführer/-in
many – viele
map – Stadtplan, Landkarte
March – März
mark – (Schul)Note
market – Markt
married – verheiratet
to match – zuordnen
may – dürfen
May – Mai
maybe – vielleicht
me – mich, mir, ich
to mean – bedeuten, meinen
meaning – Bedeutung
mechanic – Mechaniker/-in
medium – mittel
to meet – treffen
menu – Speisekarte
mess – Unordnung, Durcheinander
message – Nachricht
middle – Mitte
milk – Milch
million – Million
mini – Mini
minute – Minute
missing – fehlend
to miss – verpassen
mistake – Fehler
to mix – mischen
mobile – Handy
Monday – Montag
money – Geld
month – Monat
moon – Mond
more – mehr, weitere
morning – Morgen; Vormittag
mother – Mutter
mouse (pl. mice) – Maus
mouth – Mund, Maul
to move – bewegen, umziehen
movie – Film
Mr – Herr
Mrs – Frau
much – viel
mum – Mutti, Mama
Munich – München
museum – Museum
music – Musik
must – müssen
mustn't – nicht dürfen
my – mein/-e

N

name – Name
nasty – scheußlich, grässlich
naughty – unartig, ungezogen, frech
near – in der Nähe von, nahe
neck – Hals
to need – brauchen
needn't – nicht müssen, nicht brauchen
neighbour – Nachbar/-in
nervous – nervös
never – nie
new – neu
news – Neuigkeiten
newsagent – Zeitungsladen
newspaper – Zeitung
next – nächste/-r
next to – neben
nice – schön, nett
night – Nacht
no – nein, kein/-e
no one – niemand, nicht eine/-r
nobody – niemand
noise – Geräusch, Lärm, Krach
north – Norden
nose – Nase
not – nicht
not … yet – noch nicht
nothing – nichts
November – November
now – nun
nowhere – nirgends, nirgendwo
number – Zahl, Nummer

O

October – Oktober
of – von

Wortliste

of course – selbstverständlich
often – oft
old – alt
on – auf, am
on board – an Bord
on Fridays – freitags
on the left – links
on the right – rechts
only – einzige/-r/-s; nur; erst; bloß
to open – öffnen, aufmachen
opening times – Öffnungszeiten
opposite – gegenüber; Gegenteil
or – oder
orange – orange
order – Reihenfolge, Bestellung
to order – bestellen, sortieren
to organise – organisieren
other – andere/-r/-s
our – unser/-e
outside – draußen, nach draußen
over – über, vorbei
over there – da drüben
own – eigen/-e/-er

P

p.m. – nachmittags
6 p.m. – 6 Uhr abends
to pack – packen
packet – Päckchen, Packung, Tüte
page – Seite
to paint – anstreichen, malen
pair – Paar
paper – Papier
parents – Eltern
park – Park
to park – parken
parrot – Papagei
part – Rolle
partner – Partner/-in
party – Feier, Party
to pass – bestehen
past – nach
to pay – bezahlen
pen – Füller
pencil – Bleistift
pencil case – Federmäppchen
penfriend – Brieffreund/-in
penny (pl. pence) – Penny, Pence
people – Leute
per day – pro Tag
to perform – ausführen
person (pl. people) – Person
pet – Haustier
phone – Telefon
phone number – Telefonnummer
to phone – anrufen
photo – Foto
phrase – Redewendung, Ausdruck
piano – Klavier
to pick up – abholen, aufnehmen
picnic – Picknick
picture – Bild
piece – Stück, Teil
pig – Schwein
pink – rosa, pink
pirate – Pirat/-in
pizza – Pizza
place – Platz, Ort, Stelle
plan – Plan
plate – Teller
play – Theaterstück
to play – spielen
to play the drums – Schlagzeug spielen
playground – Schulhof, Spielplatz
please – bitte
plenty – genug, ausreichend
pocket – (Hosen)Tasche
pocket money – Taschengeld
poem – Gedicht
to point – zeigen
police – Polizei
policeman – Polizist
polite – höflich
pond – Teich
pony – Pony
poor – arm
popular – bekannt, beliebt
postcard – Postkarte
poster – Poster
pound – Pfund (Gewicht und Währung)
practice – Übung, Probe, Training
to practise – üben
to prepare – vorbereiten
present – Geschenk
to present – präsentieren
presentation – Präsentation
price – Preis (einer Ware)

prize – Preis (den man gewinnt)
problem – Problem
programme – Programm
project – Projekt
proud – stolz
to pull – ziehen
pullover – Pullover
pupil – Schüler/-in
purple – lila
to push – stoßen
to put – legen, setzen, stellen
puzzle – Rätsel

Q

quarter – Viertel
quarter past – Viertel nach
quarter to – Viertel vor
question – Frage
quick – schnell (Adjektiv)
quickly – schnell (Adverb)
quiet – ruhig, still
quiz – Quiz, Ratespiel

R

rabbit – Kaninchen
race – Rennen, Lauf
radio – Radio
rain – Regen
to rain – regnen
raincoat – Regenmantel
rap – Rap
rat – Ratte
to read – lesen
ready – fertig
real – echt
really – wirklich
red – rot
referee – Schiedsrichter/-in
regular – regelmäßig
relative – Verwandte/-r
to relax – entspannen
to remember – sich erinnern, denken an, nicht vergessen
to renovate – renovieren
to repeat – wiederholen
reporter – Reporter/-in
revision – Wiederholung
rich – reich
ride – Ritt
to ride – reiten, fahren
right – rechts, richtig, rechte/-r/-s
right now – jetzt gerade
ring – Ring
to ring – läuten, klingeln
river – Fluss
road – Straße
role – Rolle
room – Raum
round – um ... herum
rubber – Radiergummi
rubbish – Abfall
ruler – Lineal
to run – rennen, laufen
to run away – weglaufen

S

sad – traurig
safari – Safari
safe – sicher
to sail – segeln
sandwich – belegtes Brot
Saturday – Samstag
sauerkraut – Sauerkraut
sausage – Wurst
to say – sagen
scar – Narbe
scared – ängstlich
scary – unheimlich, gruselig
scene – Kulisse, Szene
school – Schule
school bag – Schultasche
to score a goal – ein Tor schießen
to scream – schreien
sea – Meer
seasick – seekrank
season – Jahreszeit
seat – Sitzplatz
second – Sekunde; zweite/-r
secret – Geheimnis
to see – sehen, jemanden treffen
to sell – verkaufen
to send – schicken, senden
sentence – Satz
September – September
to set the table – den Tisch decken
to shake – schütteln
she – sie
shed – Schuppen
sheep (pl. sheep) – Schaf
to shine – scheinen
ship – Schiff
shoe – Schuh
to shoot – schießen
shop – Geschäft, Laden
shopping – Einkaufen, Einkäufe machen
short – kurz
to shout – schreien
show – Aufführung
to show – zeigen

Wortliste

to shut – schließen
sight – Sehenswürdigkeit
silly – dumm, albern
since – seit
to sing – singen
sister – Schwester
to sit – sich setzen, sitzen
situation – Situation
size – Größe
skateboard – Skateboard
skates – Rollschuhe
skill – Fertigkeit, Fähigkeit
skirt – Rock
to sleep – schlafen
slow – langsam
small – klein
smaller – kleiner
to smell – riechen
to smile – lächeln
smoke – Rauch
to smoke – rauchen
snack – Snack, Imbiss
snow – Schnee
snowball – Schneeball
snowman – Schneemann
so – also, so, deshalb
sofa – Sofa
soft – weich
some – einige, ein paar, etwas
somebody – (irgend)jemand
someone – (irgend)jemand
something – etwas, (irgend)etwas
sometimes – manchmal
somewhere – irgendwo
son – Sohn
song – Lied
song contest – Gesangswettbewerb
soon – bald
Sorry. – Entschuldigung.
to sort – sortieren
sound – Geräusch
south – Süden
space - Platz
to speak – sprechen
special – besondere/-s
to spell – buchstabieren
to spend – verbringen, ausgeben
sport – Sport
spring – Frühling, Frühjahr
stadium – Stadion
stage – Bühne
stall – Stand
to stand – stehen
to stand up – aufstehen
to stare – starren
to start – anfangen
to stay – übernachten, bleiben
to steal – stehlen
still – noch, immer noch
stocking – Strumpf
to stop – aufhören, anhalten
story – Geschichte
storyteller – Erzähler/-in
straight – gerade
strange – merkwürdig
street – Straße
stupid – dumm
style – Stil
subject – Unterrichtsfach, Subjekt (Grammatik)
suddenly – plötzlich
sugar – Zucker
suitcase – Koffer
summer – Sommer
sun – Sonne
Sunday – Sonntag
sunglasses (pl.) – Sonnenbrille
sunny – sonnig
sunshine – Sonnenschein
super – super, toll
supermarket – Supermarkt
sure – sicher
surprise – Überraschung
sweatshirt – Sweatshirt
sweet – Bonbon; süß, niedlich
to swim – schwimmen

T

table – Tisch
tail – Schwanz
to take – nehmen, bringen, dauern
to take the dog for a walk – mit dem Hund spazieren gehen
takeaway – Imbissstube
talk – Gespräch, Unterhaltung
to talk – sprechen, reden
taxi – Taxi
tea – Tee
to teach – unterrichten
teacher – Lehrer/-in
team – Mannschaft, Team
to tell – sagen, erzählen
temperature – Temperatur
tent – Zelt
text – Text

text message – SMS
to text – eine SMS schicken
thank you – danke
Thank you very much. – Vielen Dank.
that – das
the – der, die, das
the others – die anderen
the same – derselbe, dieselbe, dasselbe
the woods - Wald
theatre – Theater
their – ihr/-e
them – sie/ihnen
then – dann
there – dort, da
these – diese (hier)
they – sie (pl.)
thing – Ding, Sache
to think – denken, glauben
third – dritte/-r/-s
thirsty – durstig
this – das, dies, diese/-r/-s
those – diese (da), die (da), jene
thousand – tausend
through – durch
to throw – werfen
Thursday – Donnerstag
ticket – Fahrschein, Eintrittskarte
tidy – ordentlich
to tidy up – aufräumen
time – Mal, Zeit, Uhrzeit
tin – (Konserven)Dose
tiny – winzig
tip – Tipp
tired – müde
title – Titel, Überschrift
to – an, zu, nach
today – heute
together – zusammen, miteinander
tomorrow – morgen
tonight – heute Abend, heute Nacht
too – auch
tooth (pl. teeth) – Zahn
torch – Taschenlampe
tourist – Tourist/-in
towards – auf...zu
towel – Handtuch
tower – Turm
town – Stadt
toy – Spielzeug
tractor – Traktor
tradition – Tradition
train – Zug
trainer – Turnschuh
transport – Verkehrsmittel
to travel – reisen
treasure – Schatz
tree – Baum
trip – Ausflug
trouble – Schwierigkeiten
trousers (pl.) – Hose
true – richtig, wahr
truth – Wahrheit
to try – versuchen, probieren
Tuesday – Dienstag
tunnel – Tunnel
turkey – Truthahn
Turkish – türkisch, Türkisch
turn – an der Reihe
to turn – abbiegen
tutor – Klassenlehrer/-in
tutor group – Klasse

U

uncle – Onkel
under – unter
underlined – unterstrichen
to understand – verstehen
unhappy – unglücklich
uniform – Uniform
unit – Kapitel
until – bis
up – oben, nach oben, hinauf
upstairs – oben (in einem Gebäude)
us – uns
to use – verwenden
useful – nützlich
usually – gewöhnlich, normalerweise

V

vegetable – Gemüse
vehicle – Fahrzeug
very – sehr
to visit – besuchen
visitor – Besucher/-in
voice – Stimme
volleyball – Volleyball

W

to wait – warten
to wake – wecken
to wake up – aufwachen
walk – Spaziergang, Wanderung
to walk – gehen, laufen
wall – Mauer, Wand
wallet – Portmonee
to want – wollen

Wortliste

wardrobe – Kleiderschrank
warm – warm
was – war
to wash – waschen
watch – Armbanduhr
Watch out! – Pass auf!, Vorsicht!
to watch – (zu)schauen, gucken
water – Wasser
water kettle – Wasserkocher
to wave – winken
way – Weg
we – wir
to wear – (Kleidung) tragen
weather – Wetter
Wednesday – Mittwoch
week – Woche
weekend – Wochenende
welcome – willkommen
were – waren
west – Westen
wet – nass
what – was
What's the matter? – Was ist los?
wheel – Rad, Lenkrad
when – wann, als
where – wo, wohin
which – der, die, das (*Relativpronomen*)
which – welche/-r/-s
while – während
to whisper – flüstern
to whistle – pfeifen
white – weiß
who – der, die, das (*Relativpronomen*)
who – wer, wem, wen
whole – ganz
whose – dessen, deren
why – wieso
to win – gewinnen
wind – Wind
window – Fenster
windy – windig
winter – Winter
wish – Wunsch
to wish – wünschen
witch – Hexe
with – bei, mit
without – ohne
woman (pl. women) – Frau
won't – will not
wooden – hölzern
word – Wort
work – Arbeit
to work – arbeiten, funktionieren
worker – Arbeiter/-in
world – Welt
worse – schlechter
worst – am schlechtesten
would – würde
to write – schreiben
wrong – falsch

Y

year – Jahr, Klasse
yellow – gelb
yes – ja
yet – schon
you – du, ihr, Sie, Ihnen
You're lucky. – Du hast Glück.
young – jung
younger – jüngere/-r/-s
your – dein/-e, euer/eure, Ihr/-e
yourselves – selbst
youth hostel – Jugendherberge

Z

zero – Null

Unregelmäßige Verben

infinitive	simple past	past participle	German
to be	was / were	been	sein
to become	became	become	werden
to begin	began	begun	beginnen
to bet	bet	bet	wetten
to blow	blew	blown	blasen, wehen
to break	broke	broken	(zer)brechen
to bring	brought	brought	bringen
to build	built	built	bauen
to burn	burnt / burned	burnt / burned	brennen
to buy	bought	bought	kaufen
to catch	caught	caught	fangen
to choose	chose	chosen	wählen
to come	came	come	kommen
to cost	cost	cost	kosten
to cut	cut	cut	schneiden
to do	did	done	tun, machen
to draw	drew	drawn	zeichnen, ziehen
to dream	dreamt / dreamed	dreamt / dreamed	träumen
to drink	drank	drunk	trinken
to drive	drove	driven	fahren
to eat	ate	eaten	essen
to fall	fell	fallen	fallen
to feed	fed	fed	füttern
to feel	felt	felt	fühlen
to fight	fought	fought	kämpfen
to find	found	found	finden
to fly	flew	flown	fliegen
to forget	forgot	forgotten	vergessen
to get	got	got	bekommen

Unregelmäßige Verben

infinitive	simple past	past participle	German
to give	gave	given	geben
to go	went	gone	gehen
to grow	grew	grown	wachsen
to hang	hung	hung	hängen
to have	had	had	haben
to hear	heard	heard	hören
to hide	hid	hidden	verstecken
to hit	hit	hit	treffen / schlagen
to hold	held	held	halten
to hurt	hurt	hurt	verletzen, weh tun
to keep	kept	kept	behalten
to know	knew	known	wissen, kennen
to learn	learnt / learned	learnt / learned	lernen
to leave	left	left	verlassen
to let	let	let	lassen
to lie	lay	lain	liegen
to lose	lost	lost	verlieren
to make	made	made	machen
to mean	meant	meant	meinen, bedeuten
to meet	met	met	treffen
to pay	paid	paid	bezahlen
to put	put	put	setzen, stellen, legen
to read	read	read	lesen
to ride	rode	ridden	fahren, reiten
to ring	rang	rung	klingeln, anrufen, läuten
to run	ran	run	rennen
to say	said	said	sagen
to see	saw	seen	sehen
to sell	sold	sold	verkaufen

Unregelmäßige Verben

infinitive	simple past	past participle	German
to send	sent	sent	senden
to shake	shook	shaken	schütteln
to shine	shone	shone	scheinen
to shoot	shot	shot	schießen
to show	showed	shown	zeigen
to shut	shut	shut	schließen
to sing	sang	sung	singen
to sit	sat	sat	sitzen
to sleep	slept	slept	schlafen
to smell	smelt	smelt	riechen
to speak	spoke	spoken	sprechen
to spell	spelt	spelt	buchstabieren
to spend	spent	spent	verbringen, ausgeben
to stand	stood	stood	stehen
to steal	stole	stolen	stehlen
to swim	swam	swum	schwimmen
to take	took	taken	nehmen
to teach	taught	taught	unterrichten
to tell	told	told	erzählen
to think	thought	thought	denken
to throw	threw	thrown	werfen
to understand	understood	understood	verstehen
to wake	woke	woken	wecken
to wake up	woke up	woken up	aufwachen
to wear	wore	worn	(Kleidung) tragen
to win	won	won	gewinnen
to write	wrote	written	schreiben

DER RICHTIGE ÜBERBLICK IN ENGLISCH!

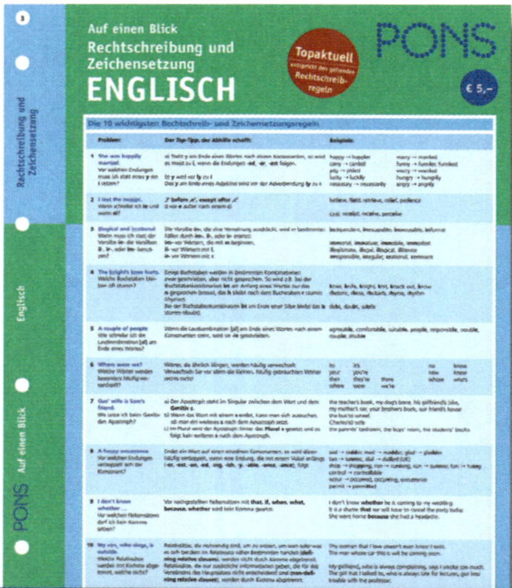

PONS ENGLISCH 6. KLASSE
AUF EINEN BLICK
Das Schuljahr im schnellen Überblick.

Grammatik, Sprechabsichten, Vokabular und Aussprache – das Wichtigste aus einem Schuljahr auf einen Blick. Für unterwegs, zu Hause und in der Schule. Mit hilfreichen Lern- und Elterntipps. Aus strapazierfähigem, abwischbarem Material mit praktischer seitlicher Lochung, passend für jeden Ordner. Für Schüler aller Schularten.
Format: DIN A4, laminiert, gelocht.
6 Seiten.

ISBN: 978-3-12-**561022**-4

PONS SCHAU NACH – BLICK DURCH!
SCHULGRAMMATIK ENGLISCH
Alle Regeln, die du wirklich brauchst.

Die Grammatik für die gesamte Schulzeit in einem Buch: alles leicht und verständlich erklärt. Mit vielen Beispielen für richtiges Anwenden. Einfach nachschlagen – schnell die richtige Antwort finden – mit vielen Tipps zum Vermeiden typischer Fehler und zu Besonderheiten der Grammatik.
Format: 5 x 21 cm, 128 Seiten.

ISBN: 978-3-12-**561393**-5

PONS

www.pons.de